POPULAR
CARD GAMES

HOW TO PLAY AND WIN

POPULAR CARD GAMES

HOW TO PLAY AND WIN

By

B. H. WOOD, M.Sc.,

and

F. R. INGS

Eighteen Favourite Card
Games for Two or More
Players, with Rules and
Hints on Play

W. FOULSHAM & CO. LTD.

LONDON • NEW YORK • TORONTO • CAPE TOWN
SYDNEY

W. FOULSHAM & CO. LTD.
Bennetts Close, Cippenham, Berks., England

ISBN 0–572–02001–5

Printed in Great Britain at
St Edmundsbury Press Ltd., Bury St Edmunds, Suffolk

CONTENTS

INTRODUCTION

SOME games, like chess, possess an ancestry that goes back for thousands of years. Other games, like those of cards, are more modest, and have only been played for a few hundreds of years. But chess appeals only to the few who have a great deal of leisure to study and practise. Card games, on the other hand, may be easily learned, and can be played at odd times. Another great advantage of card games is that the number of players can vary and that several people can join in. This little book gives instructions in playing many games, some for two players, but mostly for more. It will be assumed that little is known of cards, so that anyone reading this may be able to play though they may never have tried before.

An ordinary pack of cards consists of fifty-two cards, arranged in a series of four suits, thirteen of each. The suits are spades ♠ , clubs ♣ , diamonds ♦ , and hearts ♥ . The best card is the ace; following which, in this order, come the king, queen, jack, ten, nine and so on, down to the deuce (or two) which has the lowest value. For some games there are additions made to the pack, for other games some of the cards are taken out. For example: the poker pack has a joker, a fifty-third card, added. This is the most valuable card, as it can be made to represent anything, an ace or a king or an extra ten or jack or whatever is wanted. For euchre the joker is used, but all the small cards, from two to seven, are thrown out. Usually the various suits all have the same value; no ace, for instance, is worth more than any other ace; but in some games, notably bridge and its variations, the suits rank in the order spades, hearts, diamonds, clubs. These points will be explained fully as we go on.

Cards are generally dealt one by one to each player after being shuffled (that is, well mixed together) by one player and cut (some taken from the top and placed underneath) by another player. The dealer deals the first card to the player on his left, and so on, clockwise; the last card then falls to the dealer. The first player is generally the one who receives the first card. A trick is a round of cards in which each player plays one. The winner of the trick is the player who plays the best card, the ace being the highest, the king the next best, and so on. The trick winner is usually the player who leads for the next trick. An important rule is that if a suit is led, that is, put down as the first card in that round, all players with cards of that suit, say diamonds, must play diamonds. There are penalties if a player does not do this.

In some card games there are 'trump' suits. One suit is chosen, the particular game decides how this is to be done, and any card of that trump suit will beat any card of any of the other suits. For example, if clubs are trumps and the king of diamonds is played, the two or three of clubs will beat it. But a trump can, of course, be beaten by a larger trump. No player must trump a suit—diamonds, for example—if he holds a diamond. He must follow suit. If he has no diamonds he *may* trump, but if he wishes to, he can throw away a card of another suit. This is called to 'discard'.

Many games are played for points, which are scored either on a board or a writing pad, whilst the game is being played, and then counted at the finish. The value of the points in money, if a little gamble is on, is arranged before starting. In other games counters or chips, a name first used in America, are used, for which a value also has to be agreed. The counters or chips are bought at the start, so many for five or ten pence, or one penny, however you want. When the game is finished the counters are exchanged again for cash. This saves the bother of changing money as each trick is played. In other cases the stakes are played for and paid over in cash as each game is finished. In some of the more important games—whist, bridge and auction, for example—the first two games won by the same players out of three games are called a rubber. For winning the rubber there are usually extra points or stakes, which are decided by everyone before the game starts.

Jack	Queen	King	Ace
Clubs	Diamonds	Hearts	Spades

The suits rank in this order in Bridge, Spades being highest.

NAP

NAP is a good fast game for three or more players up to seven. Five makes the best number, as then the cards which are being used make about half the pack, five cards being dealt, singly, to each player. It is usually played for so much a trick, a penny, or less or more, as may be agreed amongst the players. Counters or chips can be used for convenience, bought from time to time from one player acting as banker, and 'cashed in' with him at the end of the game.

With five cards dealt in turn, one at a time to each player, you can see that the most tricks that can be made by any player is five. To make five tricks is something of an achievement. This is called making 'Nap' or 'getting the lot!' Because it is difficult to do, the player is allowed odds of two to one. That is, if he makes 'Nap' (all five tricks) he is paid by each player twice the stake for each trick. Making five counts ten. Generally it is agreed to count 'Nap' as twelve. Thus, if the stakes are a penny a trick, the player who makes 'Nap' gets twelve pence from each of the others. If he loses he pays out six pence each. This is the essence of the game of 'Nap': each player, for each hand either 'pays out' or 'receives.' The player who tries to make the tricks is the caller. All the others combine to beat him.

To determine the 'call' is the first thing to do. The dealer calls last, the player to his left calls first. The call then goes round the board. If the first player does not want to call, if he thinks he cannot make two or more tricks with his five cards, playing against all the other players, he says 'pass.' It is then the next player's turn to call. Let's suppose that he holds cards that he thinks will make three tricks—he calls 'three.'

9

The next player, unless he can make a higher call, must say 'pass.' Suppose he does so, but that the dealer, whose turn now comes, calls 'four.' As the highest caller, he is entitled to lead. The lead in Nap is doubly advantageous, because the *first card led always indicates the trump suit*.

Now take the example of five players in this instance. Twenty-five cards will have been dealt. There are then twenty-seven, to make up the fifty-two, left in the pack. There is, therefore, just a little more than an even chance that any given card will be left in the pack and not actually dealt out. If our dealer, who has called 'four,' for example, has in his hand the king, queen, ten and five of diamonds and the ace of clubs, there is about an even chance that the ace of diamonds will be in the pack and not dealt. As it is his own lead he plays the king of diamonds. Diamonds then become trumps. The ace has been dealt out, and the next player to the dealer puts it on the caller's king. The first trick then goes against the caller. He has to make all the others – he is 'top-weight.' Each player lays down their card in front of him, the winning card being turned over. The winner of the first trick now plays a heart. As the caller has no hearts, he may trump. He is now the last player, and if the trick comes in to him without being trumped previously he can take it with his five of diamonds. He then plays again, this time the queen of diamonds; the queen draws, on this second lead of trumps, the jack of diamonds. The caller has now made two tricks. His ten of trumps is bound to 'make' for his third trick. He has now one more trick to make, and he leads the ace of clubs. This card can only be beaten by a trump, but as no trumps were played to the ten which he led, he knows that he is safe. The caller has made 'four,' and each of the other players pays him four stakes. If there had been a small trump left in one of the hands to beat the caller's ace of clubs he would have 'gone down,' and would have had to pay each of the other players four stakes.

An absolutely sure hand at Nap is ace, king, queen, jack, ten, as these are the highest cards in order. But Nap is often called, and made, on hands of much less value. It depends largely upon the number of players. If only three are playing there will be fifteen cards dealt, with thirty-seven remaining in the pack. The odds are now just about two and a half to one that a given card will be in the pack, and not dealt. By the law of averages this means that in seven hands the trump ace or king will be in the pack five times, whilst it is only twice dealt out. *The smaller the number of players the greater will be the value of the cards that are held*. With seven players considerably more than half the cards will be dealt. It is then evident that the odds are in favour of the particular card being dealt. It would be foolish to risk a Nap, with seven playing, if the king was the best card in the hand.

But when there are a number of players, the caller has the advantage in the splitting up of the trumps. Let us take five players again. There are twenty-five cards dealt, rather less than one-half; there will also be, on the average, about half of the trump suit dealt, say six or seven cards at the most—thirteen cards to the suit. If the caller has three trumps this leaves four amongst the other four players. If two are without trumps this means two each to the others. If, then, the caller can win the two first tricks, any trump will make a third trick. If the caller still has the lead an ace is as good as a trump. From this it will be seen that a good 'three' hand is ace and king of trumps, and an ace of another suit, or a small trump.

One kind of 'four' hand has been described above. Another would be, say, an ace and four small trumps. The ace being led would make. The second, the smallest trump, would be beaten, but it would draw the remaining trumps from the other players' hands, and the caller would make his three last tricks. It must not be understood from this that there are never three trumps out against a hand, with five players; there are sometimes even four trumps. But generally one can reckon on two trumps against the caller only in any particular hand. Any four small trumps will usually make two tricks for this reason. Two leads of trumps are given and lost to the caller and the others 'make.' Now, as we usually only expect to get two, or at most three, trumps against a call, an ace, king, ten, one other small trump and another ace will usually make Nap. The jack and queen of trumps, if dealt to other hands, will perhaps fall to the first two tricks, and if there be a third trump against the caller it is beaten by the ten on the third round. If the first three rounds are trumps, an ace and a king of another suit will complete a Nap. An ace and queen make a good run for the double stakes, and even an ace and jack are always worth a run with five players.

Don't forget that small cards may be made trumps by a first lead and big ones of other suits used to take tricks. In this way, a hand may consist of the five, seven and nine of clubs, and two other aces, or an ace-king. This is a 'three' hand by making the clubs trumps. The first club is led and lost. The next lead is up to one of the aces. This makes. Another trump is led and lost; this clears all the trumps, leaving two winning cards in the caller's hand. If the ace or king he holds is 'led to', he wins with it and plays his trump. If anything else is led, he trumps it and plays his winning card for three.

A 'two' call is ace and deuce of trumps and another ace. The best play is ace, which wins, then the second trump, which loses, and wait for the right lead. Some players think differently, and lead the second ace. If this is trumped, which very often happens, there is little hope for the small trump making. In playing against the call, be careful to allow as many players as possible to play after the caller. Thus, if the caller plays a small card, let this be beaten, if possible, by the player last after the caller. When he leads again the caller perhaps has to trump, and if there are three to play after him, one or other of them

12

may be able to over-trump. If the caller has only one more trick to make, lead trumps. It is then the 'table' against his trump. If the caller has only a small trump left there may, by chance, be another left a little larger, which will beat it. In these circumstances, if a trick is already beaten and you hold a trump yourself, take the trick with a higher *suit* card, if you hold it, and lead the trump.

In most games of Nap it is usual to allow a player the choice of the top card if he goes Nap. It may be that he will pick up a small trump, and can then exchange a doubtful fifth card for it. If a player looks at the top card he *must* go Nap. Each player is entitled to a call, so if Nap is called before it comes to the turn of the dealer or other player, it is usual to allow Double Nap. Generally the stakes are doubled for that round. Nap, then, if the stakes are a penny a trick, is twenty-four pence from each player, if won, and twelve pence paid out to each player if the caller 'goes down.' In the case of a 'pass' all round it is usual to double the stakes for the next hand or until a call is won. A call of two, three, or four, is therefore doubled if made after a complete pass. A 'pool' or kitty is made by each successful player paying into it the agreed stake, a penny, two pence or three pence which is allowed to accumulate for the first Nap which is made. Then the kitty starts again. It is often worth while to risk a Nap which you would not otherwise call if the kitty is a big one. There are variations of the game in which conditional calls, of Wellington at double stakes, and Sir Garnet, for treble stakes, are allowed. In the latter case it is usual to deal another five cards and allow a hand to be made up from the ten for the call—the loser pays in full in this case.

A call is sometimes played of 'misère,' over a 'three,' but under a 'four,' in which all the tricks have to be *lost*. It is paid for as a 'three.' This is a popular variation and calls for and develops considerable skill.

Sometimes trumps are still recognised when 'misère' is called—sometimes the hand is played without trumps.

This point should be agreed in advance. If trumps are recognised, the caller should of course lead a suit of which he only has a single card.

Generally speaking, low cards are essential to a 'misère' call. But one or even two quite high cards need not always deter the player.

So a hand consisting of two of spades, two and ace of diamonds, three and four of hearts could be played in the following way: lead two of spades; this trick is practically bound to be taken by another player. The trick winner—let's suppose—leads clubs. Having none of these, the caller can 'throw away' the dangerous ace, and feel reasonably certain of losing the rest of the tricks in view of his very low cards.

If by chance the first trick winner leads diamonds, the two can be played to lose the trick, whilst the ace may be thrown away later. For if you have none of a particular suit, it is likely that one of your opponents will have rather more than usual of them, so you are fairly sure of having opportunities to throw away dangerous cards!

When playing against a 'misère' call, remember that the caller's weakness, if he has any, will be in his holding two cards or more of the same suit—one perhaps fairly high. Therefore do not change the lead if you can help it. Try again with the suit in which he has just successfully lost a trick.

Another variation is called 'Purchase' Nap. This is an extremely good game and well worth trying. After the dealer has dealt, and before anybody starts calling, the dealer goes round again in turn, and serves out fresh cards from the pack in exchange for as many cards as the players may wish to throw away from their original hands. For every fresh card exchanged in this way, the player has to pay one penny (or more, according to the stakes) into the pool. He must not exchange cards more than once in each round, but he can 'purchase' any quantity up to five. The cards thrown away are not shown, nor used again till the next deal. The dealer must sell to each player in turn, and to himself last, after which the calls start from his left in the usual way. In view of the extra number of cards brought into the game, Purchase Nap should be kept to a table of not more than four players, and for the same reason the calls should be made on much stronger hands than at ordinary Nap.

WHIST

WHIST could be called the king of card games. Though an element of chance enters into all card games, this happens less in Whist than in many others. Card games are all a combination of chance and skill. Even when chance predominates, great skill in playing the game will make up for a lot of bad luck. This is especially true of Whist, where a large amount of scientific play or deduction can be employed. Whist is a game for four players, though three may play it, one hand being used as a dummy partner. All the cards are dealt one at a time and the four players are alternately partners and opponents.

To determine the partners, each player draws a card from the pack. The two highest play the two lowest. To determine the deal the lowest card is taken, either in that draw, or the deal is drawn for again. The ace is the lowest card for only in this case (in all others, the ace is the highest card). Two players may challenge two others. In this case they become partners if the challenge is accepted. To decide upon the trump suit the last card dealt is 'exposed', or turned over. But this has the disadvantage of showing one of the trumps that is contained in that hand. For this reason, sometimes a second pack is cut and a trump card exposed for the whole round.

Each four cards played constitute a trick, so there are thirteen tricks in a hand at Whist. After each side gets six tricks, the 'odd trick' is scored as 'one' towards game. If one side gets nine tricks, and other side four only, 'three' are scored towards game. The 'game' is five tricks, made either in a succession of 'hands' or in one 'hand.' The winners of two 'games' out of three win the 'rubber.' In fixing stakes for play, it is usual to have 'something on' the game and an additional stake on 'the rubber.' It can be arranged to have points as well, if you want, for the tricks. So one could have a penny or two pence per trick, three pence or five pence on the game, and five pence or ten pence on the rubber. But Whist is played without any stakes at all more often than not. The score can be quite easily kept on paper or on a cribbage board.

It is important, even imperative, to remain silent while playing Whist. It would be quite unfair to give your partner any verbal indication of the cards you hold. But in the play of the hand it is a good idea to give him all the information you can. How well or how badly the last few tricks will turn out for you depends on the skill with which you can do this and on your ability to remember all the cards that have been played in the course of the hand. Skilful play and good memory will often retrieve a bad position for you. It must be remembered that all the cards are out, and that, in the long run, luck will be about equal. The best players win at Whist. With a really bad pair of hands you must expect to lose. How much you lose will depend largely upon your play.

The player next to the dealer, on his left, leads. The winner of that trick leads for the next trick. A card of the suit led must always be played if you hold it. A revoke—failing to play a suit—entails a penalty of three tricks lost. Now the partners at Whist are alternated. If it is your lead, one of your opponents will play immediately after you, your partner next, and your other opponent completes the trick. Two cardinal rules at Whist are, return

16

your partner's lead, and, as third player, play high. There are very rarely exceptions to these rules. From this it follows that you should, if leader, play first the suit that you want returned. Supposing you have only a single small club, and diamonds, of which you have three, are trumps, you lead your club. Your opponent having say, ten, jack and queen of clubs, puts on the queen, your partner holds the ace. This he puts on; the fourth player completing the trick with a small club. Your partner gathers up the trick. He has fulfilled the first rule by playing high. Now he only holds some little clubs. But he plays one of these. The next player holds king and another club. His partner put on the queen as second player. He therefore infers, and rightly, that his partner holds the jack and plays a small club. As you have no other club you now trump the trick with your smallest diamond.

It is your turn to play again. You may hold some small spades or good hearts. It can be inferred by everyone that your weak suit will be your partner's strong one. Leading a small spade, the ace and queen may be on your left. The second player would not play his ace—he probably would not put on his queen. You partner holds the king, jack and two other spades. You have asked for his highest card, and he plays the king. It wins and he returns your club, which again you trump. This makes up four tricks for you, but two of your trumps are gone and two of your partner's best cards. You return the spade lead, but the player next to you wins the first with his ace and the second with his queen. Now three leads of four have been played to spades so that one only remains unplayed. Two leads of clubs have been played, but only seven cards of that suit have fallen. There are, therefore, six more clubs to come.

As the game progresses you gather information by watching the fall of the cards. Your opponents 'get in' with their spades and follow up with trumps. They win two rounds of trumps on the second of which you have to

17

throw away a card. Your partner notices that this is a heart. The third round of trumps he 'makes' with the queen of diamonds, and then leads a heart. You play your highest, win the trick, and return the heart lead. He takes the trick and then leads the last spade. This forces the remaining trump from your opponent's hand, and so the game proceeds.

In Whist the combinations of hands are almost endless. Rarely is it seen that two hands exactly alike turn up. The chances against holding, for example, all thirteen trumps runs into millions to one against. A hand that is sometimes held, but very infrequently, is one without a card in it higher than a nine in any of the suits. This is called a Yarborough. A famous sporting nobleman, Lord Yarborough, was always willing to bet a hundred pounds to a shilling that any hand dealt at whist would be better than this. Lord Yarborough won many shillings. But though the combinations are almost endless, the average hand at Whist runs to a fair sprinkling of court cards; aces, kings and queens, amongst the smaller ones. For playing many of these ordinary hands there are various rules which have been found useful in practice. 'Lead from your strongest suit' is perhaps the best. A strong suit is, of course, that in which you hold most of the winning cards—not necessarily all of them.

There are many laws in Whist which govern the etiquette of the game. Most of them are concerned with points that do not often arise but may do so and so have to be anticipated. What is more important for the player is to have some general instructions as to how to play hands of various kinds. These are given later. It must not be thought, however, that these are laws; they are just general directions which most good players adopt. If you follow them your partner will have some idea of the nature of your hand. In the early stages of a game such information is very valuable. One term used at Whist finds a place here. It is 'finesse.' It is used to describe the winning of a trick by an inferior card when another, better, perhaps the top, card is in hand. As an example: if your partner leads diamonds from two cards, an eight and four, and you as third player have an ace, queen, seven and six, you would 'finesse' the queen if you played it on the first round and the second player held the king. This looks to be against the rule 'third player play high.' But you must be governed always by the exact cards you hold. In this case you would return your partner's lead with the ace, and then give him a small diamond on the third round so that he could trump.

Finesses are of two kinds, speculative and obligatory.

The finesse speculative is as follows: you hold ace, queen; or ace, queen, jack of a suit, which your partner leads. Third in hand, you play the queen, if you hold ace, queen; or jack if you hold ace, queen, jack. This play is adopted on the chance that the king is to your right, and is therefore a speculation.

The finesse obligatory is as follows: you hold king, ten, seven, and three of a suit, and you lead the three; your partner plays the queen, and wins the trick, and returns a small card of the suit. From the fact of the queen winning, you know the ace is not held by your right-hand adversary; you also know your partner does not hold the jack. When your partner returns a small card of the suit, you know he does not hold the ace. If both the ace and jack are to your left, it does not matter whether you play king or ten third in hand. If, however, the jack is to your right, your ten draws the ace, and you remain with the king, the best card of the suit. So you are *obliged* to play the ten third in hand in order to give yourself one chance—that is, that the jack is to your right; consequently, this is called the finesse obligatory.

The following rules are what is considered 'correct' and safe play in all the circumstances mentioned. A beginner would do well to memorise them, and in fact every player should make them the basis of their play.

The reasons for them will soon become apparent to any beginner who plays frequently enough—and by following them they will avoid exasperating their partner!

AS FIRST PLAYER

Holding, in plain suits—	First Lead	Second Lead.
Ace, king, queen, jack	king	jack
Ace, king, queen	king	queen
Ace, king, and others	king	ace

Holding, in plain suits—	First Lead	Second Lead.
Ace, king only	ace	king
King, queen, jack, with one small one	king	jack
King, queen, jack, and more than one other	jack	king, if five; queen if more than five
Ace and four or more small	ace	fourth best of those remaining
King, queen, and others	king	if king wins, fourth best of those remaining
Ace, queen, jack, with or without one small one	ace	queen

Holding, in plain suits—	First Lead	Second Lead.
Ace, queen, jack with two or more	ace	jack
King, jack, ten, nine	nine	king, if ace queen falls
King, jack, ten	ten	
Queen, jack, ten, nine	queen	nine

20

Queen, jack, and one small	queen	
Queen, jack, and two or more	fourth best	

In trumps:—

Ace, king, queen, jack	jack	queen
Ace, king, queen	queen	king
Ace, king, and five others	king	ace
Ace, king, and fewer than five small	fourth best	

AS SECOND PLAYER

Holding—	*Card led*	*Play, second hand.*
Ace, king, queen	small	queen
Ace, king, jack	small	king
Ace, king, and others	small	king
Ace, queen, ten, etc.	small	queen

Holding—	*Card led*	*Play, second hand*
Ace, queen, ten, etc.	jack	ace
In trumps	small	ten
Ace, queen, and small	small	small
Ace, jack, ten, etc.	small	small
In trumps	small	ten
Ace and small	small	small
King, queen, jack, etc.	small	jack
King, queen, etc.	small	queen
Queen, jack, ten, etc.	small	queen
Queen, jack, and small	small	jack
Ace and small	queen	ace
King and others small	queen	small
King and one other	small	small
Queen and one other	small	small
Queen and one other	Jack or ten	queen

21

AS THIRD PLAYER

The third player plays his best card except when: (1) the second player plays a card higher than any card held by the third hand—the lowest card is then played; (2) a sequence is held, such as king, queen, jack; queen, jack; ace, king, etc.—then he plays the lowest or lower card of the sequence; (3) a 'finesse' is obligatory or desirable.

AS FOURTH PLAYER

The last player has to take the trick if he can—provided that his partner, the second player, has not already taken it. If so, or if he cannot take it, he throws away his most useless card.

BRAG AND POKER

BRAG is a simple form of poker, and is a good introduction to the latter. Both games are essentially different from the 'trick-taking' games already described.

The play consists of betting that your hand is better than your opponents', and if none of them is willing to take your bet, the cards are not shown at all! This of course rarely happens; there will almost always be someone to take a sporting chance.

The values of various hands are reckoned according to the comparative frequency with which certain combinations of cards are met with when dealt round in the usual way from a shuffled pack.

You will appreciate that in a hand of five cards, four aces are a very rare occurrence. This being so, four aces is an extremely valuable hand in Poker. Other combinations are valued according to their rarity or otherwise.

Let us take Brag first as being the simpler game. Three cards make a 'hand' at Brag. It is agreed beforehand whether three cards only shall be dealt to each player, or whether each shall have five dealt, two of which are discarded before play commences. This last method makes the best game.

The hands rank in the following order of value:—

1. *Three of a kind*, sometimes called 'pair royal' or 'triplet.' Three aces of course beats three kings; and so on.

2. *Running Flush, i.e.*, three cards of the same suit in numerical order. Ace, king, queen, beats king, queen, jack; and so on.

3. *A run, i.e.*, three cards of any suit in numerical order. Four, five, six, beats three, four, five; and so on.

4. *A Flush, i.e.*, three cards of the same suit, in any order. The highest card of a flush determines its value compared with other flushes. So, a flush containing an ace beats one containing lower cards. If the highest cards in two flushes are of the same value the next highest card is referred to.

5. *A Pair, i.e.*, two cards of a kind, as two queens, two fives, of any suit. A pair of tens beats a pair of nines, and so on.

Note that all hands coming into one of the groups numbered above beat all hands coming into a lower group; *e.g.*, the smallest run will beat the biggest of flushes.

Having learnt their values, let's begin to play!

The player on the dealer's left has first bet. He bets whatever he likes (or nothing at all—in which case he says, 'I drop out') that his hand is better than anyone else's. If it is a valuable hand he will bet fairly high. But not *too* high, or he may get no takers. Let us suppose he bets three pence. The next player may 'come in' if he thinks his hand is as good as the first player's. The first player having placed his stake in the pool, those that 'come in' must each place a like amount.

But the third player may be confident that he holds the better hand; if so, he may 'raise' the stakes, saying, 'I raise it to six pence.'

If he does so, all those who 'come in' after him must stake an equal amount.

The 'raising' will probably cause the fourth or fifth player, who perhaps has a weak hand, to say, 'I drop out.' The turn in this way comes round to the original caller again. If he is still confident that he holds the highest hand he may say, 'I raise another three pence'—paying *six pence* into the pool. If, on the other hand, he is not so sure, he may pay three pence to make his stake equivalent to the third player's. If this happens the hand is at an end. Those that have 'come in,' and remained in, will show their hands and the one who has the highest taking the pool.

But the call may go round several times if someone 'raises' during each round. Those who want to remain in the game must make their stakes equivalent to the raiser's— or else make a further raise. Often all players but two drop out—and the hand ends by one player making his stake up to that of the raiser in order 'to see' the 'show-down' as it is called.

At first sight it may seem that success is a matter of pure chance. Not so; a good player will keep in mind the probabilities of his hand being likely to have a serious rival— according to whether there are many or few players. As explained in the section devoted to 'Nap,' and as all 'Nap' players will know, if only half the pack is in use then it will be, roughly speaking, about even chances as to whether a given card is in play or not.

Furthermore, the good player will save, and on occasion make money by careful study of his opponents. There are many people who cannot conceal the fact that they have good cards or *vice versa*. People's behaviour varies of course according to the individual, but by watching, certain useful indications will make themselves apparent!

On the other hand, a skilful player will cultivate methods of misleading opponents, who, it must be remembered, are watching for 'signs' as to the *real* value of the hand that is being betted on.

POKER

POKER probably possesses more variations than any other game. So much so, that before beginning to play it is necessary (and customary) to first discuss exactly how the game will be played. 'Draw Poker' is the most commonly played variation, followed probably by what is known as 'Whiskey Poker.' But even these variations may be played in different ways, so that no player should consider that the variation with which they are familiar is 'correct' or necessarily the best way of playing.

In Poker the hands are valued in the same manner as at Brag. But as a 'hand' is five cards there are more possible combinations, and they run in slightly different order of value. The hands are:—

1. *Straight Flush, i.e.,* running flush of five cards.

2. *Fours, i.e.,* four of a kind, as four aces, which make the highest 'four.'

3. *Full house, i.e.,* a pair royal (three of a kind) *and a pair*. The value of the pair royal decides the winner as between two 'full houses.'

4. *A Flush*. Five cards of the same suit. The highest card or cards decide between two flushes.

5. *A Straight*. Five cards in numerical order, of any suits. Ace may be counted as high *or* low, *i.e.,* as a 'one' or as an ace.

6. *Threes*. A pair royal, as three sixes.

7. *Two pairs*. The highest pair decides between two or more hands of this type.

8. *A Pair*. Two cards of same value; a high pair beating a low pair.

If two or more hands should be equal as far as their main cards are concerned, as for instance two hands of two pairs, sixes and sevens, then the odd card becomes the deciding factor. This principle applies throughout. If two hands are exactly equal, the pool is divided. Some players give value to the suits (as we said in the Introduction), and in this method no two hands can be equal.

The joker may be used if you want. Experts players think that it does not improve the game since it brings in too great an element of chance. If used it may be counted as *any card in the whole pack* by the player fortunate enough to receive it. The highest hand when the joker is in use is five aces.

DRAW POKER is usually played as follows:—

Five cards are dealt to each player. Five players make the best game, but from three to seven may play. It is an old-established rule that if a card falls face upward in the deal, it must be accepted.

Before play begins, two things must be agreed on, the 'limit,' which is the maximum amount by which any previous bet may be raised, and the 'ante,' a small fixed stake which the 'age,' the player on the immediate left of the dealer, must put up before seeing his cards.

The hands are now dealt out. If any player now wishes to draw, he must put into the pool twice as much as the original 'ante'; he can increase the stake if he wishes, and then each player to his left, round to him again, must then at least equal this bet, or throw in his hand. The dealer gives himself his own 'draw' cards, but he must announce how many he is taking, so that all the others can hear.

It can be seen that hands may be greatly improved by 'drawing.' If on the first deal you receive a pair and three indifferent cards, you will, of course, discard the latter and draw three more in the hope of turning the 'pair' into a 'three.'

But the 'draw' is more useful than this. By watching how many cards each player takes, you may receive a fair indication of what he commenced his hand with. It is, for example, pretty certain that a player who draws three cards already holds a pair. The expression on his face may indicate whether he has 'improved' or not. Again, a player who draws one card may have either 'fours,' or the 'makings' of a 'flush,' a 'straight,' even possibly a 'straight flush'; or he may have two pairs—which are the 'makings' of a 'full house.'

So—beware of the player who draws one card, and look at him closely. He either has a very good hand, or one that is worthless or nearly worthless. If he bets cautiously, he has probably got the card he wanted and wants as many players as possible to 'come in.' If he bets fiercely, he is perhaps 'bluffing'—trying to make you think he 'has them' by a display of confidence!

After all players have 'drawn' (and you have kept a careful note of who has done so), the player on the dealer's left may bet or 'open,' as it is called. If he does not want to do so, the privilege passes to the next; and so on. Betting is usually as described for 'Brag'—but there are many variations—some of which are rather complicated. The method should be agreed on before play commences.

The reader will have gathered that 'bluffing' is a great part of the game. It is done in many ways other than the naïve scheme of plunging in heavily on a hand worth nothing.

You may bluff your opponents by drawing only one card when you hold, say, a 'three.' They will think you hold 'two pairs' or a 'broken' straight or flush. In these circumstances you stand a chance of a brisk contest with an individual who holds two high pairs, who has decided that you did not 'improve' and that his pairs will beat yours anyway.

Your 'threes' will, of course, make him lose heavily if he is a *very* decisive sort of person.

Even if you attempt a bluff, on nothing, and get found out, it is not all lost. A little later on, when you really have a good hand, you will find perhaps that a larger number than usual of your opponents will 'pay to see' your hand, because they think you may be bluffing again! Conversely, if you have had a succession of really good hands and have won several 'pots'—then a 'bluff' in the nature of a good confident bet will often scare all the others 'out'—and you scoop the pool.

You should note that unless someone 'pays to see' your hand, they have no right to see it, and you should not show it.

'STRADDLING' consists of doubling the 'ante' before the deal, and 're-straddling' is a repetition of this process. Some schools allow any players after the 'age' to 'straddle' and 're-straddle' within the limit. It is a pure gamble, with the odds against the 'straddler.'

Nearly all modern Poker is a development of 'Draw Poker' called sometimes 'Jack-pots,' which possibly puts the 'mathematical' player at a disadvantage. A player can only open, after the 'ante' and deal, if he holds a pair of jacks or better; otherwise he must pass. Once the 'jack-pot' has been opened, others may come in, even if they passed before (*e.g.* holding king, queen, jack, ten of hearts, and eight of clubs, a player could not open, but would come in and draw to his straight flush as soon as anybody else opened). The betting is then exactly as before, except that, if no one 'antes' against the 'age,' *i.e.* no one is prepared to come in by staking twice the 'ante,' every player contributes to the pool an amount equal to the 'ante,' and the next deal begins.

At the end of a jack-pot hand, the opener is required to 'exhibit' or show the cards on which he opened, whether he has won or lost. If it is found that he had no right to open, he is severely penalised (he must retire from the game, and must put up a jack-pot equal in value to the one he opened in error). One peculiar set of circumstances has caused a lot of controversy. If a player holds, say, eight, nine, ten, jack of hearts, and another jack, he can open, but will want to discard his odd jack and draw to the flush. But then he will not be able at the end of the hand to show the two jacks on which he opened. It is a good idea to have no discards gathered in or mixed together until the hand is over. The odd card can then be retrieved and exhibited whenever necessary.

WHISKEY POKER is a simple form of the game suitable for a low number of players. Each player puts in the pool an agreed amount by way of 'ante.' Five cards are then dealt to each player, with an extra hand, known as 'the widow.' The first player may either play his own hand, pass, or take the widow. If he adopts either of the former alternatives, the next player has a similar option and so on till someone elects to 'take the widow.' He takes the spare hand, and lays his own on the table, face upwards. The next in order is entitled to take in either of the exposed cards, discarding in its place one of his own, which is added to the remaining four on the table. The next player has a like choice, and so on round and round, till some player is content with his hand, which he signifies by a knock on the table. Each of the other players may still make one more exchange, after which the hands are exposed, and the best hand takes the pool.

Should any player knock before the widow is taken, the five cards are turned up, and each player (other than the one who knocked) has one draw from them. Should the round of the table have been made without anyone taking the widow, the five cards are turned up, and the players draw from them in rotation until someone says they are satisfied.

There is no 'raising' or betting on the hands, the stakes consisting solely of the amount originally placed in the pool.

A few general hints on play round off this introduction to Poker.

Don't pay to draw unless you have at least a 'pair' or higher, in the original deal. It has been said that if you go in on a pair of face-cards only, in the long run you will come out better than those players who go in on smaller pairs. This might be too cautious a game to be popular at a social table. At any rate, never pay to draw if your hand consists merely of mixed worthless cards.

Don't waste money on drawing five cards or four 'to an ace.' The odds are enormously against your success. Avoid betting on 'two-pairs'; to new players, especially if the pairs are 'picture cards,' the hand looks good. It is practically worthless unless there are only say three players.

Remember always to watch what your opponents draw—and their subsequent behaviour. Success largely depends on this, but do not get into habits, *e.g.*, of bluffing when you are winning lots of money, or when you have lost a lot. It will soon be noticed, and you will pay for it. On the other hand, watch for habits in other players; you may be able to take advantage of it.

Always keep cool: never lose your temper, either with those you are playing, or, more particularly, the cards.

Too much curiosity is ruinous. All the money saved at Poker comes from not seeing. It is best never to show your hand at all, unless, of course, paid to do so, and to remain silent in regard to its merits. A few people can put their opponents off the scent by a misleading line in patter, but they are in the minority. For the vast majority of players there is nothing more effective or easy than solemn mystery.

Always weigh up the odds against the cards you are looking for turning up (but don't try to calculate them exactly, this may have dire consequences for the game!). Go for the big thing whenever you have the chance, but remember that half a loaf is better than no loaf at all! So, from a hand consisting of two aces and the seven, eight, nine of a suit, discard the last three; three aces will win most poker hands, but your seven, eight, nine will be lucky if they find both the partners they want to form the straight flush.

CONTRACT BRIDGE

CONTRACT has developed from Auction, just as Auction developed from Bridge-Whist and Bridge-Whist from Whist. Once it was usual to regard Contract simply as an offshoot from Auction, which the beginner was encouraged to learn first. This no longer holds true. Contract is now firmly established as a separate game, and is by far the more popular of the two. The following explanation should allow even a newcomer to cards to play it with some hope of success and without needing to bother his head about Auction.

The essential rules of Contract are as follows:—

(1) *Paragraphs 3 and 4 of the Introduction apply.*

(2) *The game is played by four people; two play as partners against the other two, each pair constituting a side.*

(3) *The deal is decided by cutting, ace ranking high, the suits ranking, as between cards of equal value: Spades (highest), Hearts, Diamonds, Clubs; and the highest card winning.*

(4) *Bidding begins when the deal (thirteen cards, singly, to each player) has ended. A bid is made by specifying any number of tricks from one to seven inclusive, together with the name of a suit or no trump, thereby offering to contract that with such suit as trump, or with No Trump, the bidder will win the specified number of tricks over six.*

(5) *Bidding begins when the deal ends, and ends when all four players pass; or, after a bid by one of the players, when the other three players in succession pass. The dealer either makes a bid or passes. Thereafter each player in turn to the left must either pass or bid.*

(6) *Every successive bid must be higher than the previous bid.* A bid of a greater number of tricks ranks higher than a bid of a less number. When two bids are of the same number, they rank: No-trumps (highest), spades, hearts, diamonds, clubs.

A player may 'double' an opponent's bid or 'redouble' his double, providing no other bid has intervened.

(7) *When his turn comes in the bidding, if a player does not bid, double, or redouble, he must pass; this he does by saying: 'No Bid.'*

(8) *At close of bidding, the highest bid becomes the contract. The player who first bid the suit or no-trump becomes Declarer, his partner Dummy.*

(9) *When the contract has been decided, the player on the Declarer's left leads; Dummy places his cards face upwards on the table, and Declarer plays Dummy's cards for that hand in addition to his own.*

(10) If Declarer makes his contracted number of tricks, his side scores for them 'below the line.' If he makes any additional tricks, they score as over-tricks 'above the line.'

(11) *If Declarer fails to make the contracted number of tricks, his side scores nothing for tricks. His opponents score for as many 'undertricks' (above the line) as he falls short of his contract.*

(12) A 'game' is won when one side makes 100 points below the line. *A game may be completed in one hand or more.* Each side starts the next game from zero. When a side has won one game it becomes 'vulnerable.'

(13) *A rubber begins with the draw for deal and concludes when one side has won two games. The side with the greater nett number of points, above and below the line, is said to have won the rubber.*

(14) *For merely holding certain cards, 'honours,' a player may receive a bonus. In no-trumps, the honours are the aces; in a suit call they are the ten, jack, queen, king, ace of trumps.*

(15) *A grand slam is the contracting for and obtaining of all thirteen tricks; a small slam, twelve.*

HINTS ON PLAY

First and foremost, experience of actual play is essential. A dozen rubbers among players of any class will do to initiate a beginner into general procedure; from then onwards he should try only to play with good players.

Contract is much more exact and mathematical than other card games. There are many guiding principles which should be memorised from the start and this alarms some people, but they can rest assured that the hours of enjoyment doing so guarantees amply makes up for the trouble of assimilating them.

All correct bidding is based on 'honour trick' values. A suit consisting of a king and a small card may or may not, in the subsequent play, be good for one trick—all depends on the position of the ace that suit. The maker of the first bid, the 'opening bidder,' has no indication of the where-abouts of the ace, so gives his K,x the rough value of half-a-trick. Some other honour trick values are included here; they can all be worked out on common sense lines:

$\frac{1}{2}$ Trick: K,x; Q,J,x.   1 Trick: K,Q; K,J,10.

$1\frac{1}{2}$ Tricks: A,Q; K,Q,J; A,J,10.

2 Tricks: A,K. $2\frac{1}{2}$ Tricks: A,K,Q.

These values are all very conservative (thus, K,x is more likely to take a trick than not) and are likely therefore to hold good even when the other side has most of the good cards. In each case, x represents a small card of the same suit.

Opening bids fall into three classes:

(a) Holding three or more honour-tricks, call 'one' of a suit or no-trumps according to the distribution of high cards among the suits. If you have honours in all four suits, call the latter, otherwise call your longest suit.

(b) Holding four or more honour-tricks and a very long suit (but not unless) so that you can take at least seven tricks with that suit as trumps, call 'three.'

(c) Holding five or more honour-tricks, bid 'two.'

Under all other circumstances, say 'no-bid.' Here are some specimen hands and bids:

(1) ♠ K,8,2, ♥ A,Q,6, ♦ K,Q,4,2, ♣ 10,4,3. Total, 3 Honour-tricks: One no-trump.

(2) ♠ K,Q,J,9,7, ♥ A,Q,2, ♦ 10,9,6, ♣ 5, 4.
Total, 3 Honour-tricks: One spade.

(3) ♠ K,J,10, ♥ K,5,3,2, ♦ Q,J,9, ♣ A,10,8.
Total, 3 Honour-tricks: One no-trump.

(4) ♠ K,8,2, ♥ K,Q, ♦ K,10,9,4, ♣ K,10,9,4.
Total, 2½ Honour-tricks: No bid.

(5) ♠ K,J,10, ♥ 9,5,3, ♦ K,9, ♣ A,Q,10,8,7.
Total, 3 Honour-tricks: One club.

(6) ♠ 2, ♥ A,K,Q,10,4,3,2, ♦ 7,6,5, ♣ A,Q.
Total, 4 Honour-tricks: Three hearts.

(7) ♠ J,10,6,2, ♥ A,K,Q, ♦ Q,7,6,5, ♣ A,Q.
Total, 4 Honour-tricks: One no-trump.

If the next bid is made by an opponent of the opening bidder, it is called an 'over-bid,' and can be made on a minimum of 1½ honour-tricks, *e.g.* on the following hand, 'one spade' could be bid over 'one club,' 'one diamond,' or 'one heart':

♠ A,J,9,5,3, ♥ 6,4, ♦ K,8,3, ♣ 5,4,2.

If it is necessary to call two in order to over-bid, an extra honour-trick is required. After 'one spade' the following hand would justify a call of 'two diamonds':

♠ 6,2, ♥ K,Q,5, ♦ A,J,10,6,2, ♣ 5,4,2.

In reply to a partner's opening bid, if you have four cards of his suit, or three to the queen (or a higher honour) and two outside honour-tricks, call 'two spades.' For every extra trick over this holding you can call one more. Holding:

♠ Q,7,3, ♥ A,K,2 ♦ K,7,6, ♣ K,5,3,2, you could raise him to 'three.' When supporting your partner in a suit, but never in making a bid of your own, count a blank suit as two tricks, a 'singleton' suit as one trick. Holding:

♠ K,6,5,4, ♥ K,7,6,3,2, ♦ A,Q,9,8, ♣ none, you can raise a bid of 'one spade, heart, or diamond' to 'four.' Always use your judgement in making a supporting call; never hesitate to call a five-card suit of your own, or to bid no-trumps if your strength lies outside your partner's suit.

To return to opening bids. Perhaps once or twice in an evening's play you may be dealt a hand like this:

♠ A,K,6,5,4, ♥ A,Q,8,5,2, ♦ A, ♣ K,10.

Even if your partner's hand is worthless, you are practically certain of making game. But if you call at once, four spades, he may have a singleton spade, and six to the jack in hearts. It is necessary to find the safest and best call—it may even be no-trumps. You do this by calling *two* spades. An initial call of two has a special meaning: it is a 'forcing bid'; it absolutely *forces* your partner to keep the bidding alive until game is reached.

What if your partner makes a 'forcing call'? You must respond as follows: Holding a worthless hand—less than one trick—bid two no-trumps. NEVER PASS. If you have a good suit yourself, call it. If you have one and a half tricks outside your partner's suit, call three no-trumps.

On a hand with three or more honour tricks, you may respond to an ordinary opening call ('one') from your partner, at any time, by a 'forcing raise.' You must not bid his suit, or no-trumps; but a bid in any other suit, of one more than necessary, is a forcing bid. Your partner must then keep the bidding open until game is reached by rebidding his own suit, bidding some other suit, or bidding no-trumps if he has no other suit. Thus he may open 'one spade' on ♠ K,9,7,6,3, ♥ 2, ♦ A,Q,4,2, ♣ K,Q,8; if you then force with 'three hearts' he says 'four diamonds'; and if you then say 'four hearts' or 'four spades,' his duty has been done.

As stated, no-trump bid in this connection is never forcing. If you wish to force in this way you must bid a suit. Also no 'game' bid is forcing. If you have already

36

CONTACT BRIDGE SCORING TABLE

	Odd Tricks Bid and Won in	undoubled	doubled
TRICK POINTS FOR CONTRACTOR	Clubs or Diamonds, each	20	40
	Hearts or Spades, each	30	60
	No-Trump { first	40	80
	{ each subsequent	30	60

Redoubling doubles the doubled points for Odd Tricks.
Vulnerability does not affect points for Odd Tricks.
100 Trick Points constitute a Game

		not vulnerable	vulnerable
PREMIUM POINTS FOR DEFENDERS/CONTRACTORS	**Overtricks**		
	Undoubled, each	Trick Value	Trick Value
	Doubled, each	100	200
	Making Doubled or Redoubled Contract	50	50
	Undertricks		
	Undoubled, each	50	100
	Doubled { first	100	200
	{ each subsequent	200	300

Redoubling doubles the doubled points for Overtricks and Undertricks, but does not affect the points for making Doubled Contracts.

PREMIUM POINTS FOR CONTRACTORS/HOLDERS	**Honours in One Hand** { All Honours	150
	{ Four Trump Honours	100
	Slams Bid and Won { Little, not vulnerable 500, vulnerable 750	
	{ Grand, not vulnerable 1000, vulnerable 1500	
	Rubber Points { Two game	700
	{ Three game	500

Unfinished Rubber—The Winners of one game score 300 points
  If only one side has a part score in an unfinished game, it scores 50 points.
Doubling and Redoubling do not affect points for Honours, Slams, or Rubber.
Vulnerability does not affect points for Honours.

scored forty below the line, two hearts, bid and made, would just give you game: therefore, 'two hearts' as an initial bid is not forcing. If you wish to 'force' under these circumstances, when a 'two' call would just give you game, you must call one more than is necessary for game, *i.e.* in this case, three hearts or three clubs. When you jump over game like this, no-trumps *can* serve as a forcing bid. The bid must be spontaneous; if the opponents over-call your four hearts by four spades you are not forcing in saying five hearts.

Slam bidding is the most interesting part of Contract; it can only be practised when the calling is quite accurate, and partners can depend on each other. The final rounds of bidding are based on an intelligent analysis of the preceding calls. The simplest slam the writer played commenced with his dealing himself: ♠ A,K,10,9,5, ♥ A, ♦ A,7,6, ♣ K,Q,9,8. He opened with two spades, and his partner, holding: ♠ Q,J, ♥ K,2, ♦ K,Q,J,8,5, ♣ A,J,10,7, called 'seven no-trumps,' and, needless to say, scored them. Assuming the forcing to have been sound, where were the five tricks? The holder of the second hand by subtraction could place them exactly, and bid the grand slam, though holding only one ace. Every slam bid is not so simple, but every one is dependent on a similar process of subtraction.

Naturally, every bid has firstly game, and secondly slam, in prospect. But this is the golden rule for Contract—Don't let either of these objects distract you from a quiet analysis of the real merits of your hand. You open 'one no-trump' and your partner puts you up to 'two no-trumps.' Oh, how you would like to go three, game! But, if you have only the bare two and a half tricks in which you first called, pass! If your partner could have gone three, he would have done so. It will surprise you to note how often you make just those two no-trumps and no more.

Again, don't assume every slam invitation is a slam command. If your partner jumps your three hearts to five, look carefully at your hand and remember your bids on it. You have bid, perhaps, once or twice, or even three times. Each of these bids conveyed an indication to your partner of some strength. Have you anything *more* to show? A row of kings and queens is an encouraging sight, but don't let them mislead you.

The forcing system contains one or two traps for the unwary. The consequences of a lapse are sometimes quite damaging. Never pass a forcing call; if you have a worthless hand, bid no-trumps. Your partner will then proceed to base his calculations mainly on his own hand: but if he has to play his beautiful hand in, say, a miserable two clubs contract, he may express himself forcefully! Also, watch the score. If you want to force, make sure you do force, and do not make a game bid. But the worst bridge crime is forcing when you don't intend to. Your partner opens one club, you holding ♠ 6,5,4, ♥ K,Q,9,5,3, ♦ K,6, ♣ 8,2 call 'two hearts,' forgetting that one heart is enough. Then any homicide he commits is justified.

'Doubling' and 'Redoubling' affect nothing but the final score. If you think your opponent is unlikely to make the contract he has bid, you 'double' him, in this way increasing his possible penalties.

THE PLAY OF THE HAND

The play of the hand is, if anything, more important than the bidding. After all, a bad bid can sometimes be saved by spectacular play, but theoretically correct bidding is useless if the caller cannot make the tricks he should.

Opening leads: Remember the bidding and try to place the high cards in the various hands. If your partner has bid, lead the highest of his suit. Holding a suit headed by A,K, which has not been mentioned in the bidding, lead the King, then your partner's suit. He will then know how to get back into your hand when he wants to. Lead the King also from a suit headed by K,Q. Avoid leading from a suit headed by a 'tenace' (e.g., A,Q). The best 'blind' lead against a suit call of six or seven is a trump. See also the leads given in the chapter on Whist.

In play, remember the evergreen maxim: 'Lead through strength up to weakness.' Thus, if cards in two suits are as follows:

```
                    ♦ K,J,9
                    ♣ 9,7,3
                    North
♦ 4,7,2    West                East    ♦ A,Q,10
♣ A,Q,10            South              ♣ 6,5,4
                    ♦ 6,5,3
                    ♣ K,J,8
```

the only way for East and West to make six tricks is for West to lead diamonds only, and East to lead clubs.

A good defensive lead is a card which the declarer must trump in his own hand, thus weakening his trump suit. One often sees beginners, when playing a hand, lead a card from dummy and trump it in their own hand. This is nearly always bad, as their small trumps will make in any case. On the other hand, every effort should be made to make use of trumps in dummy. Suppose you have:

```
          ♠ 10,9,6
          ♥ None
          ♦ 8,6,4,3,2
          ♣ 9,6,5,3,2
          (Dummy)

          (Declarer)
          ♠ A,K,Q,8,5,3
          ♥ Q,J,2
          ♦ 10,7
          ♣ Q,4
```

then the only chance of making 'two spades' is by trump-ing two hearts in dummy. Declarer should lead a heart at once not even leading out ace of trumps. In a trump declaration, however, unless there are definite reasons against it, trumps should be lead out at the earliest oppor-tunity, and cleared from opponents' hands. This is vital.

In playing a no-trump hand, play out from long suits, not from short ones, even if the latter have top honours. You thus establish low cards, which you 'make' when you regain the lead with the top honours. In defending against no-trumps, don't switch your lead from suit to suit, ham-mer away patiently at one.

We have given only the sketchiest outline of Contract bidding and play. There are exceptions to almost every rule we have quoted, and it must be understood that the above is only an 'elementary course.'

It will pay any beginner to buy one of the well-known books on Contract by acknowledged experts on the game. They will not stretch any but the slenderest purse. The minimal expense would prove worthwhile.

SOLO WHIST

THIS is a splendid game which unites the best features of Nap and Whist. Three or four players play with an ordinary pack of fifty-two cards. If three play, either three hands only are dealt, or one complete suit is withdrawn, as the players agree between themselves. When four play, the game may be individual, or as partners, according to the call. The cards are dealt three at a time. The four last cards are dealt singly, the final card, the dealer's, being turned up for trumps. This is a better method than three-three-three-four.

Stakes are usually fixed at so many points for each call, generally two for the lowest, four for the next call, six the next, and eight the highest, with, perhaps, twelve for a special call. The game is designed for individual play—for solo play—and 'solo' is the lowest individual call, for which four points are given in pence, or whatever is agreed upon. To make a 'solo' the caller has to make five out of the thirteen tricks, with the other three players against him. This looks to be quite a simple matter, but the beginner playing solo is soon enlightened! If the player calling solo makes 'over tricks' he gets points for them. If he fails to 'make' he gets penalised for each trick 'down.' For example, a player calls 'solo' and makes eight tricks—he receives four points for his solo and three more for his extra tricks. If he makes only three tricks on his solo call he is 'down two,' and pays up four for lost solo and two more for 'tricks down.'

The calls go round as at Nap, the player to the left of the dealer having first call. If his hand is not good enough for five tricks alone he may call 'propose,' which is an intimation that he has *at least four good tricks* in his hand. The next player may 'pass' or 'accept' the proposal; he will do the latter if he feels that he also may make sure of four tricks himself, or eight in all between the two players who thus become partners in the call. If nothing higher is called than this 'proposition,' play proceeds by the lead from the next player to the dealer with trumps as indicated. The two who are playing together play as they sit, next to each other or opposite, as the case may be. If they make their eight tricks, in whist play, they score two each, with added points for 'over' tricks and penalty, as for solo, for tricks down.

Solo is a call above 'propose and take,' sometimes called 'prop.' and 'cop.' Above the solo call is 'misère,' in which every trick must be lost by the player. There are no 'over' or 'under' tricks at 'misère.' It must be reckoned as made or lost. Six is paid up or paid out for it, by or to each other player than the caller, as at Nap. In solo the player next to the dealer leads. The caller does not himself lead as at Nap. To win a 'misère' is not easy unless one has two long suits, with a good share of the smallest cards, including the deuce or three and four, is short of one other suit, and 'safe' on the last. I have called a 'misère' and been beaten on the first trick in leading a five. The deuce, three and four were played to it!

'Abundance' in Solo Whist is an individual call to win nine tricks out of the thirteen. It is a fairly rare achievement, unless one holds the bulk of one suit with ace and king or ace and queen for the top, and five or six others with the jack, in addition to a couple of other aces or an ace and king of the second suit. In abundance the caller can make his own trumps. Eight points are awarded for making the nine tricks, with 'overs' and 'unders' as before. The next call, which goes over the abundance, is 'abundance royal,' that is, an abundance with the original trump suit retained. For this call ten or twelve points are generally given, as may be arranged.

An 'open misère' is a call to lose all tricks with the hand exposed after the first trick has been played. *Abondance declaré* is a call to win all thirteen tricks. The caller makes his own trumps and then leads. These calls double the ordinary stakes for 'misère' and 'abundance.'

Solo Whist is a game that needs skill and courage to win. One must be prepared to take moderate risks if you can see that the run of the cards is favourable to the caller. But the impulsive player must be careful. Luck is less in evidence in Solo Whist, perhaps, than at ordinary Whist, over a long run, or so it seems, because the player is more frequently acting entirely upon his own responsibility. His failure cannot be blamed upon his partner. If he is wise he will, however, attribute his winning more to good chance than to himself.

The following hints for play are well worth remembering:—

When you and your partner sit side by side, you should never finesse in a lead coming from him if he is sitting on your right, and if your partner and then an adversary have to play *after* you, you should win the trick with the highest of a sequence; *i.e.,* holding king, queen, put on the king, otherwise your partner will think the king is against you.

It is much better that your lead should be up to your partner than through him; although should you be proposing and accepting, this second case should not prevent your leading trumps.

It is a general principle in propositions and acceptances that trumps should be used to draw trumps in order to establish plain suits.

Never force your partner to trump if you are weak in trumps yourself.

If you have to commence the game against a 'misère,' it is wise to lead from your shortest and weakest suit, and to lead a medium card if you have one—such as six or seven—and certainly not to commence by leading a deuce, unless, indeed, it is a single card, and even then it is not always advisable.

Against other declarations it is well to commence with your longest suit.

Except under extreme circumstances do not lead trumps against a solo call. But if the caller refuses to lead trumps, an adversary should, if possible, put the lead with the player on the caller's right, to give him an opportunity of leading trumps through him.

As a general rule, your discards should be from your weakest and shortest suits. You should not, however, leave a king unguarded, and it is dangerous to leave a queen only singly guarded. With a long plain suit headed by ace, king, queen, it is sometimes advisable to inform your partner of the fact by first discarding the ace. In other cases, your *first* discard should be from your weakest suit. Subsequent discards convey no information, as they may be from strength.

While returning your partner's suit is generally a wise thing to do, you should be careful to act as far as possible upon the maxim of playing 'through the strong hand up to the weak one.'

EUCHRE

THIS is another game much played in America. It is played with a poker pack, from which the small cards, deuces to sixes, have been discarded. It is a game for two, three or four players. If four play, two can be partners, as at Whist, in the other cases—as also with four if preferred—the game is 'cut-throat' each player for himself. Five cards are dealt to each player by threes and twos at a time. Tricks are played as in Whist. After five cards have been dealt to each player, the next card is faced up on the pack to indicate the trump suit. The essence of the game is to make three tricks, to count for a point, or all five for a march, two points. Five points is the game. The first player on the dealer's left has the option of ordering the dealer, if the game is 'cut-throat'. To take up the trump card. 'I order it up,' he says. This announces his determination to play against the others for a point, or a march, three tricks, or five in all. If, after ordering the trump up, he fails to make three he is 'euchred,' and each opponent scores two against him. The first player may 'pass' in which case the option passes to the other player or to the dealer if two only play.

When it comes to the dealer's turn he may elect to take up the trump, for which he substitutes a card from his own hand. He says, 'I pick it up,' and then has to make three, or else his opponent, or opponents, score two each against him. The dealer may turn down the trump. In this case the next player may make trumps or pass. If all the players pass, there is a new deal.

If four players are playing as partners, and the first player passes, the dealer's partner, instead of ordering up, will say 'I assist.' His partner then takes up the trump and play proceeds. If they fail to make three they are 'euchred.' The dealer or his partner may 'go alone'. The other hand is then placed on the table. If a march is made 'alone' it scores four points.

The best trump is the joker. The next best is the 'right bower,' which is the jack of the trump suit. The next best is the 'left bower,' which is the jack of the other suit of the same colour. Ace, king, queen, ten of trumps, etc., then follow in order. If diamonds are trumps, the jack of that suit is 'right bower,' the second best card, and the jack of hearts, 'left bower,' the third best card. If clubs are trumps, the jack of spades is 'left bower.'

A variation of the game in England is to use the deuce of spades as a 'Benny' instead of a joker as a best card, and the deuce of hearts as a second 'Benny.' If a red suit is trumps the red 'Benny' is the right 'Benny' and the black the left 'Benny,' with bowers as before. But in this case the 'right bower' becomes the third best card, instead of the second, and the 'left bower' is fourth best card. The best rule to follow at Euchre is to practise as often as you can with the best Euchre players you can find. If strong in trumps lead them at the first opportunity. If weak, hold off. Trump play is the most important feature of Euchre.

PONTOON

ALSO known as 'Vingt-et-un,' this is almost wholly a game of chance, but there are certain principles which will materially assist a player if he knows and uses them consistently. Any number of players may take part. The full pack of fifty-two cards is used; if a lot of people are playing, two or more packs may be mixed together. The players are divided into punters on the one hand, and the dealer or banker, who pays or receives the stakes individually put up by the punters, on the other.

It is usual to shuffle the pack and cut it, and then to deal, to all the players in turn, a card or cards faced up, and to make the player who receives the first jack the dealer. But this naturally gives those who receive the first few cards an advantage, and the cut, as used at Bridge and similar games, is fairer.

Having decided who is to take the bank, the maximum initial stake is agreed. Play then begins. The dealer gives one card to each player, and finally one to himself, all face down. Each player looks at their card, and each punter places a stake, which may be anything up to the maximum, alongside it. The object of the game is to collect cards which total twenty-one, or approach as near to it as possible, without going over ('busting'). For this purpose, all court cards count ten, an ace counts one or eleven as desired, and other cards have their pip-values.

Stakes, then, are 'made' on the first card dealt. The banker, if he receives a good first card, may say 'I double you.' All stakes must then be immediately doubled.

A second card is now given to each player in turn, still face downwards, the dealer receiving his own last. Each player, including the dealer, again inspects his cards.

'Pontoon' consists of an ace and a ten or court card, i.e. any two cards which total twenty-one. If the dealer holds a 'Pontoon' he shows his cards and receives from each player double the amount of that player's stake, or four times its value if he doubled it. If, however, someone else has a Pontoon, the punter only loses his original stake, or twice it if doubled; he is said to pay 'once' instead of 'twice.'

47

Usually the dealer finds he has no Pontoon: it is then his duty to offer a card or cards if required to each player in turn.

But, first of all, anybody holding two similar cards, such as two sevens or two queens, may 'split' them. This he does by receiving an extra card on each, after which he plays them as two separate hands, starting with the original stake (doubled or undoubled, as the case may be) on each. A split *must* be announced, and the two extra cards dealt out, before the game has gone any further. The banker alone can await his turn before deciding to split. If two or more players wish to split in the same round, they receive their extra cards in turn. Splitting can be extended. If a player splits eights and receives one or both of the remaining eights, he can start a third or fourth pile.

Splits negotiated, the banker turns to his left-hand neighbour, who may wish to 'twist' or 'buy.' The former means that he receives his cards face upwards, the latter, face downwards, and, in this case, he must increase his stake by some amount not greater than what is already there. If he increases his stake by two chips, he is said to 'buy' the card for two chips, and cannot thereafter buy for more than two. After having bought in this way, he may either buy or twist further cards; but once having twisted, he is not allowed to buy on that hand.

Thus, each punter is satisfied in turn. Any punter holding Pontoon shows it to the bank and receives twice his final stake (except in the case previously mentioned, where the bank has a Pontoon also).

Each punter concludes his negotiations with the bank for that particular hand by saying either 'stick!' or 'bust!' If the last card he acquires brings him to twenty-one, or near it he will 'stick.' But if it takes above twenty-one he is 'bust'; he throws his cards face upwards on the table (usually with a smothered curse) and pays up his stake to the bank.

The banker's turn comes last, when all the punters have

either stuck or bust. His subsequent doings affect only those who have not bust. He turns over his cards and carries on as the others have done until he, in his turn, either sticks or busts. If the latter, he pays each of the remaining punters their stakes. If the former, he loses to those whose total score is more than this, but wins from the rest. The bank wins on 'evens'—if both bank and punter total seventeen, the punter pays up.

The five-card trick is now established as an integral part of the game. A player who collects five cards without busting receives double his final stake, irrespective of their pip-value. If both bank and punter get 'five-carders' on the same round, the punter pays the bank 'once.' A five-carder is as useless as any other hand against a Pontoon.

One 'bye-law' should be noted. Anybody may, of course, buy all three new cards to make a five-carder. But if, after acquiring his fourth card, his hand totals eleven or less, counting any aces as one, then no single card can bust him. His five-carder being assured, he must twist, not buy, the fifth card—he is not allowed to bet on a certainty. The following is the only correct procedure, and should always be observed: whenever a punter who has four cards decides to take another, he should lay his hand face upwards on the table. If under twelve, he then says: 'Can't bust!'; if over eleven, he says 'twist' or 'buy', according to his choice.

Nobody need twist or buy unless their hand totals fifteen or less. Their decision will rest on the value of the two cards they hold. If, for example, a punter found he had been dealt a court card and an eight or nine, he would decline a third. With cards counting, like these, eighteen or nineteen, the probability is that a further card accepted would bust him, as there are so many more cards of value above three than below. It is prudent, in fact, to 'stick' at seventeen or even sixteen, but, as, stated, sticking below sixteen is forbidden.

The bank is taken over by any punter who gets a Pontoon, except:

(1) When two or more Pontoons occur in the same round;
(2) When the Pontoon occurs in the first round of a new bank;
(3) When the Pontoon has been built up on a 'split' card. If a punter makes a Pontoon on both or all of his piles, he gets the bank however.

All the cards used in a round go to the bottom of the pack, and every time a Pontoon or five-carder is scored the pack is shuffled by the bank and cut by a punter. These two rules should be scrupulously observed. The addition of a joker, which can count as any card the holder wishes, is a distinct improvement.

An experienced player nearly always wins at Pontoon. It might seem impossible for skill to enter. The banker, for instance, appears helpless; punters busting, five-carding and scoring Pontoons while all he can do is to give them the cards they ask for. But a little thought may make a considerable difference to his fortunes. If most of the punters stick after twisting comparatively high cards, such as eights or nines, it is pretty certain they are all near to twenty-one. It will then be no use sticking at seventeen ('paying eighteens' as the saying goes); he must risk another twist. He will usually bust, it is true, but occasionally he will turn a three or four, and reap a good harvest. While you are punting, observe your neighbours' methods whenever you have a chance. Are they cautious or rash? Do they stick on sixteen, or twist? Knowledge so gained may prove very useful when the time comes for you to take the bank.

There is a lot of routine in punting. It pays, on the whole, to stick whenever possible; sticking on sixteen pays more often than not. Also, it is foolish to buy on cards that already total twelve or more, unless you only need one more card to complete a five-carder. One mistake is very common: holding ace and seven, or ace and eight, many quite experienced players twist, and some even buy, led astray by the alternative values they can assign to the ace. But, once they have twisted, they are almost certain to pass eleven, and then they have no choice, they *must* twist, and they *must* count the ace as one. The only way to utilise an ace to the full is to stick as soon as the 'seventeen-or-over' zone is reached.

Calculation of exact odds leads one at once into a bewildering maze of mathematics. Any 'system' is quickly knocked on the head when one has to take the bank, and is whirled up and down at the mercy of punters who disregard any system. By putting the maximum on an ace and the minimum on any other card, one can ensure success in the long run. But what a long run it might be!—and what an unsociable game it would make!

Sometimes most of the court cards and tens stray towards one part of the pack. This is the time to back low cards: when the tens are about, bank and punters alike will stick at twenty, and the bank will win, whereas, in the other part of the pack, five-carders, the punter's friend, are at a premium.

Extraordinary results can be achieved by carefully watching the used cards as they are gathered in at the bottom of the pack. Of course, shuffling continually changes their order, and time and time again one sees the cards one carefully memorised casually going to other punters. But the writer has seen a punter confidently *buying* on nineteen, knowing that the next card was a deuce. And a five-carder in which all three extra cards have been bought is a far more paying proposition than Pontoon.

BACCARAT

IN general principles this game resembles Vingt-et-un, the players being divided into punters or backers and the dealer. The punters sit on either side of the dealer, but cards are dealt to one only of the players on each side, who thus represents the whole of that side of the table. Nine is the highest and winning score at baccarat, eight being the next best. Court cards are equivalent to tens and tens are ignored in the game. The ace counts one only, and the other cards according to the number of the pips, deuce as two, and so on. A player, for example, holding a ten, an ace, and a four, would count his hand as five only—the tens are zero. Ties neither win nor lose, but the stakes go on to the next hand.

For play, after the dealer has been elected, several packs of cards, say four or six, of the same pattern are shuffled together. Each of the players may, if they wish, shuffle in turn. Stakes are made before the cards are dealt, face downwards. The dealer then deals the cards required in this manner: the first to the players on his right, the second to himself, the third to the players on the left. If the variation of the game is Baccarat Chemin de Fer he now gives himself a second card. If it be Baccarat Banque he deals a second card to each of the others and similarly a second to himself.

Cards are then inspected. If either punters or dealer find they hold eight or nine they must turn up the hand and declare it. The other hands are then exposed. The highest points, under nine, win, and the dealer (the banker) pays or receives the various individual stakes made on either side of the table according to how the hand of one, two, or more cards which represent that side, and which is dealt to one player only, may win or lose. The presence of eight or nine in either hand must be announced, as this completes the hand. But, if neither dealer nor punters hold eight or nine, further cards must be offered by the dealer. There are certain conventions which must be considered almost as rules.

That player on either side of the table who stakes the highest individual amount plays for his side. If his points (the total pips of his cards) be now six or seven, he will refuse. If it be less than five, he will accept. If it be five, he may accept or decline. Any other course of play, since his action influences the fate of the stakes of others, is against the recognised procedure. In some card playing circles a breach of these principles is punished by a fine, or even by making the offender pay up the stakes of the other players if they should be lost. The additional cards dealt are faced upwards.

In Chemin de Fer Baccarat the deal passes to each player in turn if the banker or dealer is beaten. If the banker wins he deals again. In Baccarat Banque, unless the dealer elects to retire, he may continue until all the cards of the three or four packs have been used. As the hands are played the cards used are gathered up and thrown into a basket in the centre of the table.

Various methods are used to determine the dealer. In Chemin de Fer the positions are sometimes drawn for by lot or cards dealt, and the players seat themselves around the table in the order thus assigned. In Baccarat Banque the bank is usually put up to auction, and the player willing to risk the greatest sum at any one turn of the cards becomes the banker or dealer. It is open to any punter in the order in which he sits at the table to stake that amount at any hand by announcing 'banco.' If he does so, the other players refrain from staking on that hand. All the winnings of the banker must remain on the table, and these, with his original 'bank,' form the maximum stake for which 'banco' may be played. If no one player in his turn goes banco, each of the players makes his own stake, in front of him as he sits, and the cards are then dealt.

BEZIQUE

THIS game with the exotic name (pronounced bezeek) is an excellent game for two players. It is played with a pack of sixty-four cards, composed of two ordinary packs from which all cards from two to six have been removed. The order of precedence in each suit is ace, ten, king, queen, jack, nine, eight, seven. The score is kept on little dials, like clocks, with movable hands; one dial records tens and the other hundreds, the game being played 1,000 up. Such scorers can be obtained cheaply, as can also bezique packs.

Bezique is unique in one respect. There are so many ways of scoring that it is almost impossible not to score. Good play consists in keeping the hand clear of too many good cards, and in going after the most paying proposition. The scoring chart is appended:

A. Double bezique	 500	H. Royal marriage (king and	
B. Bezique	 50	queen of trumps)	40
C. Sequence (ace, ten, king, queen, jack of trumps)	 250	I. Marriage (any other king and queen of same suit)	20
D. Four aces*	 100	J. Any ace or ten, or seven of trumps	10
E. Four kings*	 80		
F. Four queens*	 60	K. Last trick	10
G. Four jacks*	 40		

*All in different suits.

When diamonds or clubs are trumps, 'bezique' consists of jack of hearts and queen of spades. When hearts or spades are trumps, it consists of jack of diamonds and queen of clubs. 'Double bezique' is a repetition of bezique, which only scores if the original cards are still on the table. Of course every card is duplicated, which accounts for the weird 'double bezique' and for the fact that two players may each score 'sequence' (or, for that matter, any of the other combinations) in the same game.

There is the usual cut for deal; the dealer then gives each player eight cards in the order three, two, three. He lays the seventeenth face upward on the table; this card determines the trump suit, and if it is a seven, he scores ten. The rest of the pack, which becomes the 'stock,' he places face downwards behind it. His opponent then leads, and he follows. It is not necessary to follow suit, but a trump or a higher card of the suit led wins the trick.

The winner of the trick can 'declare' anything of value in his hand among the list above. Holding king, queen of clubs, for instance, with hearts trumps, he says 'marriage,' pegs twenty, and leaves the two cards in question on the table between him and the stock. He can play either or both subsequently, but cannot take them up again into his hand. The seven of trumps can be declared in any one of three ways. It can be played to a trick in the ordinary way (whether the player has the lead or not). It may be substituted for the trump originally placed in front of the stock, or 'shown' and taken back into the hand (but in these last two cases only when the lead has been gained). In each case it scores ten.

The winner of a trick takes the top card of the stock, without exposing it, and his opponent takes the next. He then leads to a second trick, and so forth. 'Declaration' is only allowed when a trick has been won. The winner of a trick containing an ace or a ten, pegs ten for each ace or ten in it; these points are called 'brisques.'

Cards can be used more than once in declaration, *e.g.* a jack of diamonds to a marriage in clubs, when another trick has been won, may give bezique. Three more queens could be added to give four queens, sixty. But one card cannot be used to complete two combinations at the same time. Thus, with the queens of hearts, clubs and diamonds on the table, and the king of spades, the queen of spades cannot be added to score both for four queens and marriage, one of these must be forgone. Similarly, if the five cards of sequence are laid down simultaneously, the royal marriage does not score. Nor can a card, once declared, be used again in declaring in combinations of the same class, *e.g.* a bezique queen having once been declared in single bezique, cannot form part of another single bezique.

When there is only one card left in the stock, the winner of the trick then led to scores ten for the 'last trick.' He has the last chance of declaring; he then takes the last card, and the loser picks up the exposed card from in front of the stock.

The last eight cards are played out under different rules. No more declaring is allowed; the only scoring is by means of brisques, not even the seven of trumps scores. Also, it is necessary to follow suit, and to win the trick, whenever possible. If a player breaks either of these rules, his opponent receives all eight tricks.

Bezique is not so complicated as it seems. After two or three games, anyone will find himself completely familiar with the rules. It is a game worth any time spent on it.

Over each hand lies the shadow of sequence, for it is comparatively rarely that double bezique crashes out. If, therefore, towards the end of the stock you fear that your opponent is ready to declare sequence, keep him from the lead at all costs. Play high trumps, sacrifice a royal marriage if necessary. If you yourself pick up the king or queen near the end of the stock to complete sequence, declare the whole 250 and forgo the royal marriage, unless you are certain of being able to regain the lead.

Beginners over-emphasise the value of four aces. Four kings are just as good, for any queen adds twenty to their value, through marriage. Also, after declaration it is sometimes difficult to get rid of the aces without loss. You may lead the ace of spades; it is trumped and lost, and your opponent nastily concentrates on leading spades. Ultimately you have to discard another ace so as to preserve a better card, and twenty of your hundred have been lost. Whereas the four aces, had you never bothered to collect them, would probably have yielded a safe forty in 'brisques.'

Unless you have something to declare, you do not want the lead. It is easier to gain brisques when your opponent is leading. Two queens in one suit are not of any special value, for you will never score twice for four queens in the same hand: one can always be played out, but it should not be played until there is no other card to spare. Your opponent will observe the queen, and make a mental note of the fact that you probably hold her twin, and knowledge is power for him! *Vice versa*, if your opponent carelessly plays a king or queen fairly early on, do not continue relentlessly trying for four kings or four queens if that is the card you want to complete the set. Above all do not try for four queens if one queen of hearts has already been played, and the other is lying declared in front of him.

Do not collect for four jacks when there is any hope of acquiring other combinations. Thus, from a hand holding ace, king, jack of diamonds (trumps), king, jack of clubs, queen, jack of spades, and queen of hearts, play a jack without hesitation, as the kings and queens are most likely to score for you in the long run.

There are two main scoring lines—sequence, with its royal marriage, and king-queen play. Kings and queens may score remarkably well; four kings, four queens, and three marriages may give you 220, which, with the eighty or so brisques usually obtained, is a hand well above the average. Playing to the score is helpful and sometimes amusing; if you are 900 behind and your opponent only 700 or so, lead out aces and tens whenever you have the lead. He may have no choice between discarding (which allows you to creep towards 1,000) and trumping with valuable sequence cards.

Extra brisques may be picked up now and again by

careful discarding towards the end of the stock. By getting rid of your clubs, for instance, you may enable yourself to trump ace or ten in the subsequent play-off. Incidentally if special Bezique scorers are not used, brisques are most conveniently scored by abstracting them as played, and totting them up at the end of the game. They are worth bothering about. Like pawns in Chess, or infantry in warfare, they may decide the conflict.

Bezique is an ideal game for two players, and the foregoing (in the opinion of the writer, who has pegged millions of points at the game) are the ideal rules. But there are several variations. Many people have a fixed Bezique, jack of diamonds and queen of spades, and do not require the four aces, etc., for declaration to be of different suits. Indeed, in the three-handed game, any four aces count 100, similarly for kings, queens and jacks.

RUBICON BEZIQUE necessitates another dial on the scorer, for, on a single hand, the pegging may pass 5,000. Four of the reduced packs (128 cards in all, and a bit of a handful) are used, nine cards being dealt to each player in threes. 'Carte Blanche' is introduced, the holder of a hand without a face-card receiving 50. He shows his cards one at a time and takes them up into his hand again. Moreover, he can claim 'Carte Blanche' after every subsequent trick, until he picks up a face-card.

The most distinctive features of Rubicon Bezique, however, are the 'triple' and 'quadruple' beziques, which count 1,500 and 4,500 respectively. The latter is known as the 'Grand Coup.'

The game is decided on one hand; the winner deducts the loser's score from his (ignoring fractions of a hundred, and counting any differences less than a hundred as a hundred), and adds 500 for game. If the loser had failed 1,000, the scores are added, instead of being subtracted, and 1,300 instead of 500 is added for game.

The laws of Rubicon Bezique have been standardised by the Portland Club of London. This is the club responsible for drawing up the international rules of Contract Bridge.

PIQUET

FOR long considered by many the best card game for two, Piquet has been finally standardised by the Portland Club. References testifying to its antiquity, occur in the plays of Shakespeare and his contemporaries.

The twos, threes, fours, fives, and sixes are removed from an ordinary pack, and, of the remaining thirty-two cards, twelve are dealt to each player, two or three at a time, and the rest placed to one side as the 'stock.'

The usual custom is to play for the best of an even number of hands, usually six, and to alternate the deal, for there are definite advantages for the non-dealer, or 'elder' hand. He has the option of discarding any number of cards, from one to five, from his hand, replacing them from the stock. The dealer, or 'younger,' hand can then exchange in the same way as many cards from his hand as are left.

This discarding is easily the most important part of the game, as it enables an indifferent hand to be turned into a good one. The players strive to increase their chances of scoring for one of the combinations below, and of taking tricks in the final play-off.

CARTE BLANCHE: A hand devoid of face-cards counts 10 if claimed for and shown at once.

The following scores are reckoned after the discard and replenishment from stock.

POINT: The player holding the longest suit scores one for each card in it. If the longest suits of the respective players are equal in length, the pip-value is reckoned (aces 11, court cards 10, others their face value), and the highest point is the only one that scores; if the players still tie, neither scores.

SEQUENCES: of three are called Tierces and score 3; of four are called Quarts and score 4; of five, six, seven and eight are called Quints, Sixiemes, Septiemes, and Huitiemes, and score 15, 16, 17 and 18 respectively. The only player to score for sequences is the one who holds the best, *i.e.* the longest, or if there are two of equal length, the higher; and this player also scores any others he holds. If the best sequences on each side are equal, both in length and value, nobody scores for sequences.

SETS: Sets of three or four cards higher than nine are called Trios and Quatorzes, and score 3 and 14 respectively. The lowest Quatorze beats a Trio, Quatorzes and Trios being valued among themselves by their pip value. Only the player holding the best set scores for sets, but he scores for all his sets.

Elder names the value of his point; if Younger cannot equal it he answers 'good'; if he can beat it he answers 'not good.' If he can just equal it he asks: 'how many?' Elder then works out his pip value (he need only mention the units figure of his total), and the same formula is repeated.

Elder then proceeds to name his best sequence, and finally his best set, discovering in the same way whether he can score for them or not. Point and sequence, when scored by either party, must be shown to the other, if asked for.

The Elder, having named all the winning combinations in his hand, and added up score, leads a card. The Younger now declares all *he* has to score.

In the play-off which follows, the object is to gain tricks. The second player must follow suit if he can, otherwise he can discard any card he likes. The first player to any trick counts one for the card he so plays; but, if the second player wins the trick he also counts one. An extra point goes to the winner of the last trick. If any player wins more than six tricks, he scores an additional ten; if he wins all twelve, he scores forty instead, for CAPOT.

PIQUE and REPIQUE: Any player scoring thirty before the play-off starts and before his opponent scores at all receives a bonus of 60 for 'repique.' If the Elder scores thirty, on combinations *and* play, before the other opens his score, he gets 30 for 'pique.' The Younger can never 'pique,' for his opponent scores a point for his first lead.

GAME: A Partie, as stated, usually consists of six deals, and is won by the player with the higher total score. The winner of the Partie deducts the loser's score from his own, and adds one hundred for GAME. If the loser fails to score a hundred, his score is added to the winner's, instead of being subtracted.

The first essential of good play at Piquet is good discarding. Never keep high cards simply because they are high cards; plan out definitely which point, sequences, and sets you intend to go for, and discard accordingly. It often pays to discard an ace or king; the odd card you get in exchange may complete a Quatorze or Quint. Before you finally discard, subtract your hand from pack to find out what your opponent is likely to hold. It is useless depending on a Quatorze of tens if you are completely without kings.

ELDER almost invariably profits by exchanging all five cards. He should go out, above all, for a good point; the right to lead in the subsequent play means that nearly all his point cards are good for tricks. He is definitely the attacking hand; if he holds aces in two suits, he can safely leave himself blank in the other two, a dangerous thing for Younger to do.

YOUNGER'S mission is to avoid his opponent's running away with him. If he has nothing but K, 7 or K, 8 in a suit, he should keep both, as his adversary may hold the other six, and the winning of a trick in that suit may avert a pique. Younger must never forget that he is the defender for the time being.

More urgent considerations apart, the players should go in for evenly balanced hands; a quint and a quatorze are usually more useful than two quints.

The play of the hands is a matter of mere mathematics; the players both know most of the cards in their opponent's hand. Long suits should be led in preference to short ones for the reason given in Contract Bridge, pp. 31–41.

PELMANISM

'PELMANISM' may strike some people as rather indigestible mental fare, but it makes a very pleasant change from routine games. The rules are very simple.

For two or three players, one pack is employed; for a greater number, another pack may be added.

The cards are spread face downwards on the table, the player on the left of the dealer turns over two of them. He must call out their value (suits being ignored throughout), expose them clearly to the rest, and then replace them, face downwards. If the two form a 'pair', *e.g.* if they are two sixes or two queens, he removes them as a 'trick,' and he is then entitled to expose two more cards. He can continue in this manner as long as he continues to turn up pairs, but as soon as he fails to do so, his neighbour takes his turn, and so on.

The idea is, of course, to remember the positions of the cards exposed by previous players. When all the cards have been removed as tricks, the winner is the player who has amassed the most.

The secret of success is a good memory. Every person

will develop his own private system of mnemonics. We have found it helpful to memorise the cards lying along certain paths, usually twisted in and out the main body of cards, like snakes. It is extraordinary how many cards can be 'indexed' in this manner. If one is repeating to oneself: 'six, eight, king, two, ace, five, nine,' and turn up a king, one knows that its partner is the third along the 'snake.' But, if the king is removed, it is essential to start the memorising afresh: 'six, eight, two, ace, five, nine.'

The last few tricks have the same importance as at Whist, as they usually fall in a run to the same person. So, if there are only six or seven pairs left on the table, it pays to be cautious. If your first turn-up takes you nowhere, *i.e.* if it is a seven and you are ignorant of the whereabouts of any other sevens, play for safety. Turn up a card which has come up quite recently, and which everybody knows, rather than expose a new one for their delectation!

Silence is more imperative at this game than at Whist, if it is to be played at its most competitive, but most people will prefer it in a noisier and less 'correct' garb—the more mistakes the merrier!

POUNCE

PATIENCE is well known for its peacefulness. Nobody can quarrel with himself. Yet Pounce-patience, or more simply 'Pounce,' can become the most exciting of all card games. It is probably the only one in which the young and athletic can be certain of defeating the aged and experienced, and from which those weak of heart or of eyesight should be kindly, but rigorously, barred.

As many different packs are used as there are players, and each player has one to himself throughout. They must differ in the design, or, better still, in the colour, of the card backs.

Each player deals out four cards from his pack, face upward, before him (his 'front row'), and seven more, face downward, at his side. These latter form his 'stock,' and should be in a position convenient for grabbing, on his right if he is right-handed.

The idea of the game is to build up 'piles' in the middle of the table, each containing cards of one suit only, starting with the ace and ending with the king.

At the signal to start, when everybody is ready, the players run through their remaining cards in twos, dropping the upturned cards behind their front rows. The uppermost card of any two is eligible to go on any pile, and the lower can also be played if the top one has gone. Of course, for a time, only aces will go, but as the piles grow, deuces and higher cards can be played on to them.

When a player has run through his pack, he transfers one card from back to front, and repeats the process.

What of the 'front row'? As the piles mount up, the four cards of this will become playable one after another. Whenever one is played, a card is brought up from the stock to replace it, and so on. The first player to exhaust his stock cries 'STOP' in a loud voice, and the game ends forthwith.

Now comes the business of counting the score. The other players count the cards remaining in their respective stocks, the number left being their 'debit.' They then remove their stock and front row, and all cards they have not been able to play out, from the table. The piles are now turned face downwards and sorted out according to their backs, so that each player knows how many cards he has been able to play on to them. He subtracts his debit to get his net score for that hand. Thus, if he got thirty cards on to the piles, but had four cards left in his stock, his score would be twenty-six. The game is usually played a hundred up; the winner receives a number of chips corresponding to the difference between his score and that of each loser. Thus, if the first hand to take anybody beyond the hundred leaves the scores: A, 119; B, 80; C, 102; D, 49, then A receives, from B, 39; from C, 17, and from D, 70 counters.

If a player on adding a card to a pile disturbs the pile unduly, he must tidy it up, otherwise the others are entitled to call out.

To win at Pounce, it is necessary to concentrate. Do not spare either eye or nerve! The quicker you run through your pack the more chances you have; but don't run through so quickly as not to leave yourself time for a fleeting glance round the table every few seconds. Beginners invariably forget all about their front rows. Any card played from these has a double value; it counts as one more towards the final score, and by depleting the stock, it reduces the debit. If your front row consists mainly of high cards it is particularly important not to miss a chance of playing one of them, otherwise somebody may call 'STOP' before you have reduced your stock at all. Unless the effort is too much for you, keep a wary eye on the front rows of the other contestants, too.

The 'pounce,' the distinctive feature of this game, occurs when two people (or more!) simultaneously turn up the same card, one which will go onto one of the piles. Each attempts to play his card on the pile, but one will have got there first, perhaps only by merely a hair's breadth: his card will be underneath, and the other one must be retrieved. If two fronts rows happen to contain a similar card, the nervous tension, as a pile mounts towards it, may become excruciating.

This is a good game for two people, though 'pounces' are infrequent. It is a fine game for three or four or more, and causes much hilarity. A glance at its potentialities reveals that in a school of five players a robot card player would be required to keep an eye on twenty cards on front rows, the constantly-changing pairs he puts down, and twenty constantly-changing piles. The moral of which is: 'Don't try to be a robot!'

POUNCE IN PROGRESS
(With a big 'Pounce' in view)

BLACK MARIA

THIS game, in which the malevolent queen of spades is known as 'Black Maria,' or 'The Black Lady' (and in some quarters by even more sinister titles) is, in the writer's opinion, one of the very best of card games. It has developed out of 'Hearts.' A fine game for the family, it can call for really deep thought, and rarely fails to be amusing and entertaining.

An ordinary pack is used, but it may have to be adapted according to the number of players, so that each receives an equal number of cards. If any cards have to be removed for this purpose, the nines or tens of clubs or diamonds are usually chosen.

The whole pack is dealt out as for Whist. Each player then discards two cards from his hand, passing them to his left-hand neighbour and receives in return two from his right-hand neighbour. The player on the left of the dealer now leads, and the cards are played out in tricks, just as in Whist or Nap, the winner of a trick gathering it in and leading to the next. There are no trumps.

At the end of the hand the tricks are turned up and scrutinised. Any hearts count one each against the winner of the trick containing them, and the queen of spades counts thirteen against. All the scores are negative; the winner is the player who has scored the fewest, and the best possible score is zero. Moreover, the tricks themselves have no value. One player may not take a trick, another may take ten, yet neither may lose a point.

The game is usually played seventy-one up. As soon as some player passes the seventy-one mark, the game is over, the person who has the lowest score receiving from the others according to the respective difference between his score and theirs.

In one variation, the queen of spades counts only

eleven against, and the ace, king, queen, jack of hearts
count respectively five, four, three, and two against.

We have added here some hints on play:

THE PASS-ON

If you pick up the queen of spades, but only one or two
other spades, pass her on, otherwise, after a few leads of
spades, she will win the trick. If the ace or king ac-
companies her, and you pass her on, pass that on as well.
But under normal circumstances, and whenever she is
well guarded by spades, keep her.

The next thing to examine is your heart suit. If you hold
one or two low hearts, *e.g.* 3,4, and 6, or deuce, 4,5, you
are pretty safe. You will be able to 'play under' any time
they are led. If your lowest one is higher than the six,
however, you are unsafe, and it is advisable to discard any
you can.

A good general discard, if it is not imperative for some
reason to get rid of hearts or spades, is a couple of cards
from a short suit. Thus, if dealt the following hand:

♠ 8,3,2. ♥ Q,J,5,3,2. ♦ A,6. ♣ 7,5,4.

discard the two diamonds. Bear in mine that you are to
receive two probably very nasty cards from your right
hand neighbour. By leaving your diamond suit blank, you
enable yourself, on the first round of diamonds, to discard
whatever little surprise he has in store for you.

When in doubt, pass on high hearts; never pass on low
cards if you have higher cards of the same suit; never pass
on a spade lower than the queen. The ace and king of
spades are dangerous cards to hold if you are short of
spades. Get rid of them.

THE PLAY

Caution is the key-note of the play. On the first round

or two of a new suit one is usually safe in playing high cards, but even on the second round the danger of discards begins.

When in doubt, lead low spades, unless you hold the ace, king, or queen. Holding the ace or king, never play them unless forced to, or unless yours is the last card of the trick. If you are 'safe' in hearts, *i.e.* hold several small ones, lead them. You then clear out the remaining hearts, and they will not be discarded on your tricks in other suits.

No general principle is so helpful as a careful count in each suit, particularly in hearts and spades. It doubles your chances of winning if you know how many cards of each suit have been played and which is the lowest card remaining in each. Nothing is more depressing than to see a player lead out the two of clubs, when nobody else has any clubs left, and gather a rich harvest of hearts, together with 'Black Maria.' Nothing, on the contrary, is more delightful (except to the sufferer) than to see a player deliberately lead out the queen of spades, knowing that it must be taken.

Cutting your losses is an integral part of the game. With a hopeless hand (all high cards) but many spades, lead out the latter freely. You may receive a pile of hearts, but you will eventually drive the queen out of her hiding place.

It always pays to keep back a deuce or other low card as a 'get-away,' otherwise the lead may come your way near the end of the game, and never leave you. Suppose the queen of spades, but no clubs, have been played, and suppose you hold the four last spades and ace, queen, two of clubs, you must lead out the ace and queen first, or you will be left with the lead and collect any remaining hearts. Even if you have ace, king, queen, jack and two, it is worth while leading out most of the high cards as a rule. You may pick up one or two hearts, but the person who beats the deuce will get many more.

When the first chance comes for you to discard, on the

lead of a suit in which you are without cards, exercise discretion. You may have a far better discard than a heart; perhaps the ace or king of spades, or some other high card, which may prove dangerous. Also, when you achieve proficiency, and hold a good hand, you can attempt the nicety of reserving your hearts specially for those of your opponents with the best scores. But this is a risky business, except in the hands of a really good player, and a beginner should always drop his bombshells at the first chance.

RUMMY AND COON-CAN

CONQUIEN, that noble and ancient Spanish game, has travelled widely. It crossed the Atlantic Ocean with the early Spanish colonists to Mexico. From thence it wandered into Texas, where it gave birth to its child, Rummy. Nearly a century ago, it returned to take Europe by storm; it gained for awhile as popular a place as Contract Bridge was to occupy, but it passed rather out of favour after a few years, following the corruption of its name to Coon-Can.

The object in both Rummy and Coon-Can is to collect 'sets' of at least three of a kind, *e.g.* three jacks or three fours, and 'sequences' of at least three cards in the same suit, *e.g.* queen, jack, ten of diamonds. But, since the games diverge at once, we shall consider them separately.

'ENGLISH' RUMMY

Any number of players from three to six may participate. Two full packs are shuffled and cut, the cards are dealt out singly, seven to each player, and the rest of the pack (the stock) left face downwards, except for the top card, which is exposed in front of the stock. The player on the dealer's left takes either the exposed card, or the card from the top of the stock, into his hand. He then takes one from his hand, and places it face upwards, on the top of or in the place of the exposed card. There is thus never more than one card exposed. Each player in turn does likewise, until someone calls 'rummy.' Rummy is called when the cards in a player's hand total only seven, or less. In reckoning this total, cards from two to ten count face value; court cards count ten, and aces one. *But*, all completed sets or sequences count zero.

A hand composed of three kings, two fours, a nine and a jack, would therefore total twenty-seven. A hand consisting of three, four, five, six of hearts, and three queens would count zero.

Once 'Rummy' is called, the game is over, and the score is taken. Each player is debited the value of his hand calculated in the above way. When a player's score amounts to a hundred, he is out, but he has a right to buy himself in again at one more than the next highest score. Before starting, each player puts in two chips: if the scores after (say) five hands are 61, 71, 88, and over 100, the last player can restart at 89 by putting in three more chips. Besides this, each player pays on every hand one chip for each completed ten he scores. He pays in this way two chips for 27, five chips for 51, and so on. The players are reduced by elimination, and the last one takes the pool.

Where there are three playing, and sometimes when there are four, intermediate 'buying' is allowed. Suppose A, B and C are playing, and A drops a card in front of the stock which B does not want, but which C would like to possess, as B takes the top card from the stock, C can say: 'I buy that card.' He picks it up, and must put another chip in the pool. But he has no corresponding discard; from then onwards he holds eight cards in his hand. When his turn comes, he picks up one card and discards one, just as he would have ordinarily have done.

Another variation of the game allows any other players, in rotation, to play odd cards on the Rummy-caller's completed sets, and thus lessen their scores. Thus, if he lays down three kings, the five, six, seven of hearts, and the seven of clubs, his left-hand neighbour could play the eight of hearts on his sequence. The next player could play the nine, or the four, of hearts, or another king, and so on, each lessening his score where possible. But if the second player in the above case held a nine of hearts, and the third the eight, only the eight could go on the sequence. When this final small re-adjustment has been made, the scores are assessed as before.

Usually one or more jokers are introduced. They can take the place of any cards at the wish of the player holding them, but, in the final count, peg fifteen each. More often, all deuces act as jokers, *i.e.* they can count as anything.

'FRENCH' RUMMY

Two packs and two jokers are used, but deuces do not count as jokers. The dealer deals out to himself first, so that each other player receives thirteen, and he receives fourteen cards, the remainder forming the 'stock.' He starts the game by discarding a card face upwards. The next player takes this, and discards in his turn, and so on. If a player collects sets and sequences the cards of which total fifty (jokers counting 15, aces 11, court cards 10, others their face value), he can 'show down.' He exposes them face upwards in front of him, retaining his remaining cards. Once a player has shown down, others can do the same, even if they total fewer than fifty. They can also take the top card of the stock if they wish, instead of the card just discarded—they did not have this choice before.

Whenever a player's turn comes round, he can add odd cards to the exposed sets or sequences. The winner is the player who first shows down all his cards. The (negative) scores of the other players are then reckoned as above. All cards remaining up in a hand count against the holder, however, even if they form complete sets or sequences. The only way to decrease one's liability is not only to collect such sets but to 'show them down' as well.

There is no buying of cards, or buying oneself into the game again, when once out. The game is 1,000 up, and as soon as somebody passes this mark, the player with the lowest score becomes the winner.

If a player 'shows down' all his thirteen cards in sets and sequences before anybody else has done so, he receives double stakes. If he puts down all thirteen without taking a single card, he receives double stakes, and his score goes back to zero.

COON-CAN

Through French Rummy we merge into Coon-Can. Though it strongly resembles Rummy, Coon-Can is suitable for two people, whereas this can hardly be said of the other game. With evenly-matched players it can become quite exciting.

Ten cards are dealt to each player, and one card placed face upwards in front of the stock. The players, from the start, have the option of taking the top card of the stock if they wish. Seven cards is the minimum for the first showdown, but, as in Rummy, there is no minimum for the other player. A player may add odd cards to any showdown on the table.

The winner is the first player to show down all his cards, and he scores the value of any of his adversary's cards not shown down (reckoned as in French Rummy). The game is 100 up. When showing down for the last time, a player, may, or may not, discard a card on to the pile by the stock.

In one variation of Coon-Can, a player may show down any number of cards at any time, but if the first to show down does not win the game, he loses an extra 30 points.

In both Rummy and Coon-Can, the sets must be all different, *e.g.* three sixes must be all of different suits. In Rummy, the ace only counts as 'low' in sequences, whereas in Coon-Can it can be high, low, or intermediate. Thus the sequences ace, king, queen, jack and queen, king, ace, two, three, which are allowable in Coon-Can, are forbidden in Rummy.

HINTS ON PLAY

While playing these games it is necessary to be always on the look-out for unexpected combinations of cards. A very helpful combination to go for is one of the form: ten of hearts, ten, nine of clubs; or: three of spades, three, four of diamonds. Four different cards, *i.e.* in the first case either remaining ten, or eight or jack of clubs, will complete these as sets or sequences. In English Rummy, don't buy a card unless it actually completes a set or sequence. You are increasing your liability every time you do so.

Watch what your opponent picks up. If he has eagerly seized on the seven and eight of diamonds, it is courting disaster to discard the nine.

Most of the excitement of French Rummy and Coon-Can comes through holding up a hand, even when you are entitled to show down. You may all but complete a hand after one or two rounds: why show down, when you look the probable winner, and allow your opponent to get rid of three or more of the cards that you expect to count against him? This is a perfectly legitimate argument, but don't let it completely dominate you. If the card you want does not turn up at once, or at most within a very few rounds, show down. It may be at the bottom of the stock; it may be in your opponent's hand.

FAN TAN

THERE are several varieties of Fan Tan, one of which is a gambling game of evil reputation! The kind described here is quite a good round game, suitable for playing at parties and whenever you want to play cards without being over serious.

Before describing the play, it must be said that a full pack is required, the aces rank lowest and kings highest, that every player must be provided with an equal number of counters, say twenty, that five, six or seven players constitutes the best number for providing the greatest amount of fun, and that the object of each player is to get rid of his cards as quickly as he can.

When the play is about to begin, each player puts a certain number of counters in the pool. Any number may be decided on; but two will serve very well when there are more than five participants; three, if there are less.

The dealer shuffles and the person on his right cuts. He then commences to deal, beginning with the person on his left. In some cases, the cards will not permit of being shared out equally: nevertheless, the full pack is dealt out in rotation and those who are saddled with an extra card must abide by their slight misfortune.

Play is opened by the person on the dealer's left. His duty is to put the seven of any suit, face upwards, in the centre of the table. If he does not possess a seven he pays a forfeit of one counter to the pool. It is now the turn of the person to the left of the 'deficient' player. He must oblige with a seven, and, should he be in a similar position, he, also, must pay the forfeit. So the game goes on until somebody lays a seven.

Now let us turn to the first player. If he lays a seven, as he should, the next player to his left must lay either a six or an eight of the same suit or any other seven. If he puts down a six, it goes to one side of the original seven; if he plays an eight, it goes the other side; and if it is a seven of some other suit, it goes below the first seven. Unless he can play one of these cards, he must place the same forfeit in the pool.

Should the player number two play a second seven, the person on his left must follow with a six or an eight of either of the two suits led—or another seven.

From this, it is clear that the duty of each player is to lay down a card that helps to build up the rows in sequence, without leaving a gap, or, failing that, to pay the forfeit.

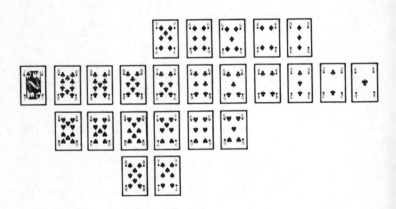

FAN TAN IN PROGRESS

The player who first disposes of all his cards takes the contents of the pool and, from all the players, a counter for each card they still possess. Then the game starts again. Each time, the new dealer becomes the person sitting at the left of the previous dealer.

There are one or two heavy penalties which must be mentioned. If anybody passes, and it is afterwards found that he could have played, he is fined three counters. Should it have been a seven that he might have put down, he must pay in addition five counters to those who hold the six and eight of the suit to which his seven belongs.

The art lies in 'holding up' your opponents. It should be said that if you hold a card in sequence, or a seven, you *must* play it; but you frequently have a choice—and an unwise choice is easy to make.

'Middle' cards in sequence are the best to hold: thus if you hold six, seven, eight, and nine of a suit, you can have two 'free goes,' as they are called, viz., the seven and eight.

The playing of these does not 'let out' any other cards, and if you can manage to play others and hold on to the six and nine till towards the end of the game, you will probably win.

The other players who hold the cards of the same suit above nine and below six can do nothing but pass in that suit until you lay one of them.

CRIBBAGE

ALTHOUGH Cribbage may be regarded as essentially a game for two players, it is adaptable for three or four. In the case of four players any two play as partners against the others, as at Whist. There are two well-known varieties of the game for playing single-handed (or cut-throat), for two or three players, viz. 'five-card' Cribbage and 'six-card,' though some players even play 'seven-card' Cribbage. To constitute a game points are scored, both for play and for the value of the hands and crib: 61 for five-card, 121 for six-card, and 181 for seven-card Cribbage. A board is used which has two lines of holes at either side, of thirty each, in which pegs of wood or of ivory are inserted. For convenience in counting the holes are divided into sets of five. Once up the board on the outer side of the line of holes, and down the inner side of the same set, with the odd hole at the end to peg game, makes 61 for the five-card game. Twice round into the game-hole, 121, for the six-card game, either single-handed or as partners. Two pegs are used, the one at the back being advanced when a fresh score is made.

A fifty-two card pack is used. The players cut for deal, the lowest dealing. The ace in Cribbage is the lowest card, counting one. The other cards rank in their proper order, up to king, and count according to the number of pips. But all court cards, save the ace, count as 'tens.' We will take first a single-handed, five-card game. After shuffling, the non-dealer cuts and the opponent deals, one at a time, five cards, beginning with the other player. Meanwhile, as a compensation for non-crib, the non-dealer scores three holes, or points. The remainder of the cards, undealt, are placed face down between the players. Each player now discards two of their cards to form what is called the 'crib,' or 'box.' This having been done, the non-dealer cuts the pack by lifting a portion of the cards. The card immediately beneath the cut is then faced up on the pack. This is known as the 'turn-up.' If it is a 'jack,' the dealer scores 'two' for 'his heels.'

In the play of the hands, points may be scored for pairs, pair-royals and double pair-royals (four-deuces, or threes, or fours, etc.), for runs of three, four, five; seven, eight, nine, etc.; and for making 'fifteen' or 'thirty-one.' For pairs two points are scored, for pair-royals, six; for double pair-royals, twelve; for runs of three or four, three or four points, as the case may be; and for making fifteen or thirty-one, two points. A single point may be made for a 'go,' that is, a player plays a card, which, with the others previously played makes the score so near to thirty-one that the other player is unable to play a further card that will not make it greater than thirty-one; the first player then scores a 'go,' one point. In five-card crib the cards are not played beyond the point of thirty-one in total score for any one hand.

Let us illustrate. A is the dealer. It is therefore B's turn to play. He plays a 'four.' Now it is evident that A cannot play any card which will make fifteen; the most he can play is a ten. We will suppose B's hand contains a four, a seven, and a nine, whilst A's contains a four, a six, and a tenth card (king, queen, jack, or ten). A four having been played by B, it is for A to consider his best play. He cannot make fifteen, but he can score 'a pair' by playing a four and saying 'eight for a pair.' He does so, and pegs two points. B replies, with his seven making in all fifteen. He says 'fifteen for two,' and pegs his two points. A now replies with his 'ten' card, saying 'twenty-five.' B cannot play, since his nine would make over thirty-one, therefore he says 'go.' A, however, has a card which exactly makes 'thirty-one,' for which he scores two points. If his card had been a 'three,' making twenty-eight, he would have scored one only for the go.

Similarly, if in the play of a hand A starts with a four, B replies with a five (very bad play ordinarily), and A then puts on a six, the total is fifteen for two, and a run of three, five (three extra points for the run). But if now B has a seven, he calls 'twenty-two for four,' the run of four (four, five, six, seven) scoring four points. It will be seen at once, therefore, that to play cards which may enable the opponent to make pairs, or fifteens, or the beginnings of runs, is bad, unless other cards are held which will enable the first player to score the pair-royal, six points, or double pair-royal, twelve points, or a run of three or four, as the case may be.

'Broken runs' are always eligible, i.e. the run scores even if the cards fall in the order four, six, five. Sometimes one card may link up a run of five or more, *e.g.* if a seven, an eight, a four and a six have been played, then a five completes a run of five.

The hand having been played, the 'show' begins. The non-dealer has the first show. The cards are turned up and points reckoned for fifteens, pairs, pair-royals, or runs in the hand, counting in with it the turn-up. Two points are reckoned for each fifteen, and the cards may be counted for fifteen as many times as fresh combinations can be made. Let us assume another hand, in which three fives are held, with a jack turned up. Now, it is evident that the three fives themselves make a fifteen. But in addition to this each of them will, in combination with the jack turn-up, make another fifteen. The score goes then thus: fifteen-two (for the three fives), fifteen-four for the first five and the jack, fifteen-six for the second five and jack, fifteen-eight for the third five and the jack. For the pair-royal six, or fourteen points in all for that hand. The other hand contains a four, five, and six. These three cards make a fifteen, that is, fifteen-two, the five and the jack score fifteen-four, and the sequence or run another three points, seven in all. Now we will assume for demonstration that with the same hands the turn-up was a five; there could not, of course, be such a turn-up, as there are only four fives and the second hand would be different, but we will let that pass. The scores would then have been, for the first hand, fifteen-eight, and twelve for the double pair royal, twenty in all. The four fives, diamonds, hearts, clubs, and spades may be counted four times in this way for the fifteen-eight; diamond, heart, club; diamond, heart, spade; heart, club, spade; diamond, club, spade. The other hand would be twelve. Fifteen-two, fifteen-four, two runs of three(six), making ten, and a pair, twelve.

When the cards of the hand, whether a run or not, are all of the same suit, the flush is counted in addition three points. In the crib a flush is only counted when the turn-up is also of the same suit. It is then five. Counting for crib, which always belongs to the dealer, follows the lines of that indicated for the hand, but as there are five cards in all to be reckoned, the points may be much higher than the hands. In discarding for crib there are two principles to be observed. Make up with the best cards you can spare from your hand, if it is your own crib; if it is your opponent's crib, throw out cards that will block her. It is evident that two cards of close value, a four and a five, or a seven and an eight, are good cards to throw into your own crib. The last two make a fifteen and only need one other, above or below, to make a run of three as well. The five is a good card to throw out, since there is very much more chance of a 'ten' card turning up than any other. To block your opponent, 'a nine and a king' are good examples. Anything that will turn up as good for one will do no good to the other. It is almost impossible to contemplate two cards of the run being thrown out by your opponent and the necessary intervening card being turned up as well to complete it.

If the hand contains the jack of the turn-up suit, 'one for his nob' is scored by the holder. In the three-handed game, if played as five-card cribbage, four cards are dealt to each player, one of which only is to be discarded. The fourth card, to complete the crib, is dealt last beside the pack. In the six-card game, whether played as a single or by partners, after 'thirty-one' or 'go' is scored, the cards which have been played are turned over, and the game proceeds as before. The first card to be played, if a seven, is seven; an eight played to it scores fifteen-two, and so on. The player who plays the last card scores one for it—'one for the last.' With six-card crib the greatest number of cards to be held, either in hand or crib, will be five, and the best score for this will be twenty-nine, made by three fives and a jack, in hand or crib, the jack to be of the same suit as the five of the turn-up. The counting then is, for the four fives together in various combinations, as

81

detailed before, fifteen-eight, each of them again in combination with the jack, another fifteen-eight, sixteen in all, twelve for the double pair-royal, twenty-eight, and 'one for his nob.'

In assessing the values of the cards to be kept in the hand, attention must be paid to three points: small cards are better for the play of the hand in making 'fifteens,' 'goes,' or 'thirty-ones'; a 'tenth' card is the most likely to turn up; odd cards are more likely to score for 'show' than even ones. No hard and fast rules, therefore, can be laid down. Each card must be considered, not only individually but in combination with its fellows, and in its relation to the prospective turn-up.

Cribbage is a game that gives ample scope for thought, and exercise for quick calculation, both in points for score, in show, and in possibilities of the play of the opponent. Practice is the secret of success in this as in nearly all card games. To assist the learner, some of the leading hands for scoring points are given as examples:—

Four threes and a nine (fifteen-twelve and a double pair-royal) 24

Three fives, a four, and a six (fifteen-eight, a pair royal, and run of three repeated) 23

Three fours, a five and a six; three sixes, a four, and a five; three sevens, an eight, and a nine; three eights, a seven, and a nine (fifteen-six, a pair-royal, and run of three thrice repeated) 21

Two sixes, two sevens and an eight; two sevens, an eight and two nines; two eights, a seven, and two nines (fifteen-four, two pairs, and run of three four times repeated) 20

Three tens, or court cards, and two fives; three threes, and two nines; three sevens and two aces (fifteen-twelve, pair royal, and pair) 20

Three threes and two sixes (fifteen-ten, pair, and
  pair-royal) 18

This score, usually a difficult one for a beginner is made
this way. First regard the three threes as nine. This, in
combination with each of the two sixes, makes fifteen-
four, the two sixes together make twelve, and each of the
threes will now make a fifteen, six extra, fifteen-ten in all.

Three fours, three, and a five (fifteen-two, pair-
  royal, and run of three thrice repeated) 17

Any three cards in sequence, with duplicates of
  two of them, but no 'fifteen' (two pairs and run of
  three four times repeated) 16

Any three cards in sequence, with one of them
  thrice repeated, but no 'fifteen' (pair-royal, and
  run of three thrice repeated) 15

CANASTA (FOUR-HANDED)

CANASTA is played with two packs of cards together
with four jokers—108 cards altogether. Most packs of
cards are sold with a joker and a blank card, and the latter
can be used as the second joker. The two packs do not
need to be of the same colour. Before the first deal they
are shuffled together.

The four jokers and the eight twos are all called 'wild
cards,' and they may be used as cards of any other
denomination. The eight threes are special cards, which
will be explained later. All the others are 'natural cards.'

The object of the game is to make 'melds' and especially 'canastas.' A meld is made when three or more
cards of the same rank—for example, three nines—are

placed face up on the table. A meld must contain at least two natural cards, and not more than three wild cards.

A canasta is a meld of seven or more cards of the same rank. It must contain at least four natural cards.

There is one exception to the rule about the number of wild cards allowed in a meld. Wild cards may be added to any completed canasta, even if it already contains three wild cards.

A completed canasta is placed on the table in a stack. The top card must be face upwards, and it should be red if the canasta is 'natural' (that is, contains only natural cards), and black if it is a 'mixed' canasta (that is, if it contains wild as well as natural cards). If a wild card is added to a completed natural canasta, it becomes mixed and the red card at the top should be replaced by a black one.

Each card has a fixed value. A joker counts 50 points; an Ace or two, 20 points; every card from King down to eight, 10 points; and every card from seven down to black three, 5 points. The red threes have a special value which will be explained later.

Cards count in favour of a player only when they are exposed on the table in canastas and melds. All the cards that are still held in his hand at the end of play count against him, their total points value being subtracted from his score. A meld or canasta is made only when the cards are placed face upward on the table, and they cannot be put down after play ends. You are not obliged to meld at any time: but if you are left at the end with, say, three eights *in your hand*, the 30 points count against you.

There are also valuable bonuses. The bonus for going out is 100; for going out concealed—that is, placing all the cards from a hand on the table at one time, in a number of melds and at least one canasta—the bonus is 200; for every mixed canasta the bonus is 300; and for every natural canasta, 500. Game is 5,000 points, with an extra bonus of 500 for making game.

Only eleven cards are dealt to each player. The remainder of the pack, called the 'stock,' is put in the middle of the table, and the top card is placed upward beside it. This is the first card of the 'discard pile.'

If this card happens to be a wild card or a red three, the next card is turned over to cover it. If more than one red three *and* one wild card are turned up, any further such cards are not placed on the discard pile, but are buried in the stock. Play cannot begin until the top card of the discard pile is a natural card. If the face card is a black three it is similarly covered before play begins.

Now the first player draws a card, which he adds to his hand; then, if he is able and willing, he melds; finally, he discards on the top of the discard pile. The next player repeats the process, and so it goes on throughout the game. Drawing is compulsory; melding is optional; discarding is compulsory except when a player goes out, when he may discard, but need not do so. Each new discard must completely conceal all the other cards in the discard pile.

If a player will have only one card left in his hand after discarding, he must announce 'one card' before making the discard. He may ask any other player how many cards he holds, and he may count the cards left in the stock.

The player must draw either the top card of the stock or the top card of the discard pile. If he takes the latter, he must also take all the cards underneath it—the whole of the pile. But this may be taken only if the top card is used in a meld, and the meld must be made at once. The correct procedure is as follows:—

The player puts the other cards for the meld face upwards on the table, together with any other melds that he is making at the same time. Then he picks up the discard pile and adds the top card to the rest of the meld on the table. The rest of pile becomes part of his hand. He makes his discard, which becomes the start of a new discard pile, and play continues.

For the first meld by a partnership the discard pile may be taken only if the player has in his hand at least two natural cards of the same rank as the top card of the discard pile.

Further, the first meld for each partnership can be made only when the meld or melds to be made add up to a minimum points score, and this depends on the partnership's score in the game so far. If they have a minus score, there is no minimum for the first meld; if they have less than 1,500 points, the minimum required is 50; if they have 1,500 or over, but less than 3,000, the minimum is 90; if they have 3,000 or over, the minimum is 120.

If, however, you wish to use the top card of the discard pile to complete a canasta as your first meld, no minimum points count is required.

A player is not obliged to take the discard pile to make his first meld. He may instead draw a card from the stock and then meld out of his own hand—but, of course, the minimum points count must still be observed unless the first meld is a complete canasta. Here, as always, cards must be melded before the discard is made.

Subsequent melds by either partner may be made either from the hand or with the top card of the discard pile; if the latter is taken, of course, the whole of the pile must be taken into the hand. There is no minimum points count after the first meld, nor is it necessary to have two natural cards to match the top card of the discard pile; one natural card and a wild card will suffice (unless the pack is frozen—this will be explained later).

In addition, after the first meld the discard pile may be taken by either partner if the top card is added to a meld already made by the side. The only exception if that the top card may not be used to add to a completed canasta. Again, this privilege is lost if the pack is frozen.

A player holding only one card may not take a discard pile consisting of only one card.

The pack is said to be frozen when any player discards a

wild card. The discard pile may then be taken only by a player who can put down two *natural* cards to meld with the top card of the pile.

The pack is said to be self-frozen if, immediately after the deal, the card turned up is either a wild card or a red three, which has to be covered in the way already explained. A self-frozen pack is regarded in the same way as a frozen pack; so that if, for example, a player makes his first meld out of his own hand, he still needs two natural cards to match the top card of the discard pile before he can take it.

The first wild card or red three that freezes the pack is placed half under, and at right angles to, the discard pile.

When a player freezes the pack the next player may not take the discard pile in any circumstances; that is, he may not take it by melding with the wild card or with the card that is left at the top of the discard pile.

At any time during the play a player may, after drawing a card and before discarding, add natural and wild cards to the melds already made by the partnership. In this way melds can be built up into canastas. When a player takes the discard pile he may use any cards in it to add to his side's melds (including the meld that he has just made with the top card of the discard pile) immediately before discarding. But he cannot *change* cards in melds or canastas *e.g.* he cannot substitute a natural for a wild card.

A few words may now be said about red threes. These are bonus cards, although they may also be penalty cards.

After each deal, the first thing each player does when it is his turn to play is to put down on the table, face upwards any red threes he may hold, and draw an equivalent number of cards from the stock. Subsequently, when a player draws a red three from the stock, he follows exactly the same procedure.

When a player takes a discard pile that was self-frozen by a red three, he places that red three on the table, but does not draw a replacement from the stock.

If a player fails to draw a replacement for a red three when it is his turn to play, he loses the right to that replacement. If he fails to place a red three on the table at the first opportunity, he may correct his mistake when it is his next turn, without penalty. But if the hand ends before the correction is made, he loses 500 points for each red three in his hand.

When play ends, each partnership that has melded is awarded 100 points for each red three that either partner has placed on the table; if all four red threes are held by one side the bonus for these is 800 points. However, if a partnership has not made even one meld—which means that all the point values in their hands will count against them—then the bonus for red threes (100 for each, 800 for four) is also *deducted* from their score.

Black threes also are special cards, but no bonus attaches to them. A black three is a 'stop' card. When it is discarded it may not be picked up by the next player in any circumstances—not even if he holds two black threes in his own hand. But a black three does not freeze the pack. Its effect lasts for only one turn in the game.

Black threes may be melded only by a player when he is going out. Even then they may not be melded with a wild card.

A player is said to go out when he melds every card in his hand, with the exception of one that he may want to discard, although he is not obliged to do so. A player may not go out until his side has made at least one canasta or unless he is making a canasta in going out.

Before melding or indicating a possible meld, a player can ask the question, 'Partner, may I go out?' If he asks the question before drawing, he may draw from either the stock or the discard pile. He does not have to ask the question before going out, but if he does so his partner must reply either 'Yes' or 'No,' and his answer must be carried out.

If a player melds any card and then asks the question,

he must go out whatever the answer. If, after asking the question but before getting a reply, the player melds or gives any information—or if his partner says 'No,' but gives any information—then either opponent may demand that the player either does or does not go out.

If, as a result of asking the question, a player is obliged to go out but states that he cannot, he has to place all his cards on the table, melding where he can; and all the cards that are unmelded are considered as penalty cards.

Penalty cards remain on the table, face upwards, until play ends. The player can treat them as part of his hand for the purpose of melding or taking the discard pile, and they may thus be used by themselves or with cards remaining in the player's hand. When the hand ends, unmelded penalty cards are counted as in the player's hand. At each turn to play, the player must discard one of his penalty cards, until such time as all of them have been either melded or discarded.

When a player draws the last card of the stock and discards without going out, the next player may take the discard. If he does not, play ends. If he takes the discard, play ends with his discard. If he does not go out, then the hand ends, the scores are counted, and there is no going out bonus.

If a player takes the top card of a discard pile and finds he cannot meld it, he is penalised 50 points and the card is replaced. If, in drawing from the stock, he sees or exposes any cards, he must show them to all the players and replace them. The next player may shuffle the pack if he wishes.

If a player mixes the discard pile with his hand before melding the top card, his entire hand must be placed face upward on the table. The discard pile is reconstructed as far as possible—with the opponents making the decision on doubtful points—and the player's original cards become penalty cards.

A meld is said to be illegal if a player puts down cards

for a first meld with an insufficient points count; if he puts down cards that are inadequate to take the discard pile (e.g. one matching card and a wild card when the pack is frozen); if he puts down all his cards for going out after having got the answer 'No' to his question, 'Partner, may I go out?'; or if he tries to go out when his partnership has not got one complete canasta and he cannot make one.

If attention is drawn to an illegal meld such as one of the above before the player concerned has discarded, he may correct his mistake—if he can—by rearranging the melds or adding more cards. Any cards that are not made into a legal meld become penalty cards.

If the next player completes his play before attention is drawn to an illegal meld, there is no penalty, and the illegal meld is regarded as if it had been legal; so a first meld with an insufficient points count would be held a correct meld.

If a player draws from the stock out of turn, at his next turn he must discard without drawing, and he is penalised 100 points. If he tries to take the discard pile out of turn, any cards he has put down become penalty cards, and he is also penalised 100 points.

At the end of a hand each side adds up its score. It is reckoned in two parts: firstly, the basic score of bonuses (for canastas, red threes, and going out), less any penalties; secondly the point score, being the points value of all melded cards less the points for cards left in the hands.

Here is the Canasta scoring table:

BONUSES		POINTS VALUES	
Natural canasta	500	Joker	50
Mixed canasta	300	Ace	20
Red three	100	Two	20
Four red threes on one side	800	King, Queen, Jack,	
Going out	100	10, 9 or 8	10
Going out concealed	200	7, 6, 5, 4, or black 3	5
For the game (5,000 points)	500		

NOTE: The 200 bonus for going out concealed is instead of, not in addition to, the 100 for going out.

Canasta can also be played as a partnership game by five or six players, or without partners by two or three players. A fuller description of the game, with advice on playing tactics, is given in *New Card Games For You To Play*, by Charles Roberts, published by W. Foulsham & Co. Ltd.

Here are some other Foulsham books which you may find useful and enjoyable.

New Book of Patience Games

Racing to Win
by Statistician

Your Lucky Number
by Steven Culbert

Reveal the Secrets in Doodles
by Patricia Marne

Travel Games for Kids
by Andrew Langley

Opening doors to the World of books

**Book Tokens
can be bought and
exchanged at most bookshops**